First published in 2001 by Booth-Clibborn Editions
12 Percy Street, London W1T 1DW, UK.
www.booth-clibborn.com
Compiled by Booth-Clibborn Editions, Scarlet Projects and Bump
Project managed by Scarlet Projects
Words by Claire Catterall
Design and art direction by Bump
Photography by Howard at Flash
Specials logo by Ian Wright
Edited by Liz Farrelly

The information in this book is based on material supplied to
Booth-Clibborn Editions. While every effort has been made to
ensure its accuracy, Booth-Clibborn Editions do not under any
circumstances accept responsibility for any errors or omissions.

A Cataloguing-in-Publication record for this book is available from
the publisher.

ISBN 1-86154-220-8

Printed and bound in Hong Kong by Dai Nippon

Facing page, Happy Light by James Goggin

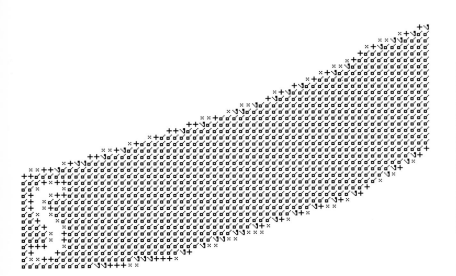

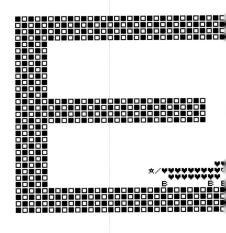

SEX PISTOLS
36PT
FROM ALBUM "NEVER_MIND_BOLLOCKS"/DESIGN BY JAIMY REID

P
PHILLIES
36PT
LOGO_OF_BASEBALL_TEAM
★×

E
EUROSTILE
48PT_EXTENDED_TWO
OUTLINE FONT (TYPE1)

It's ten years since the publication of Typography Now, the book from Booth-Clibborn Editions that heralded the digitalisation of typographic design, and spawned generations of student copyists. That unprecedented review celebrated a time of fundamental change, resulting from the adoption of the Apple Macintosh as the universal design tool, and undoubtedly gave designers more and instant freedom to experiment. A decade on, now seems an appropriate moment to look at the creative state of play within graphic design.

Since that unprecedented technological shift, and the pros and cons debates that went with it, some designers have been retracing their steps in an attempt to cut down to size the over-arching influence of digitalisation. They've done this in a number of ways; mainly by "mucking around with" and undermining the digital aesthetic itself and by incorporating traditional design techniques and hands-on skills back into their practice. Slick computer-generated design is now being tempered with a more human(e) aesthetic by way of a reacquaince with the awkwardness of manual operation.

Specials brings together a body of work that reflects these new concerns and practices; and the key to much of it lies in the processes and languages of communication. Some pieces of work result from simply taking stock of the myriad messages that crowd our everyday lives; by designers observing the things that others take for granted and editing them to reveal something new, for instance in Alex Rich's Almost/Nearly project, where observations are "lifted", or perhaps stolen, to become "work". A photograph of a road sign is entitled "Airplane", drawing our attention to the shape and form of the graphic; a fence punctured with paper cups

left by builders assumes a strange, graphic beauty when photographed in isolation. Together the group of photos, which include an Austrian picnic lunch and a Swiss road sign prohibiting flower picking, reminds us that the details of our everyday landscape hold much magic when reappropriated as a means of non-verbal communication.

In some examples the subject matter being borrowed is more directly related to the processes of communication. Thus the language of obsolete technology (computer print-out paper and punch cards), the iconography of instruction manuals (for long defunct gadgets), and the vernacular of wholesale and mail order catalogues and "kwik print" stationery, crop up as visual samples. Paul Elliman's work examines the idea of hijacking communication devices, whether projector test cards or a ouija board. In the same vein, Friendchip use the language of electricity for the record company 13amp's website; but more than simply adopting the imagery, the interface necessitates that the user "plug-in" to access information. Implicit in such appropriations is the desire to explore the deeper implications of formulas, systems, icons and "the message".

Designers are also using process as well as content to communicate meaning; unravelling it, taking an idea back to its root and building it up again, all the while keeping the process itself transparent. Combined with an exploration of different techniques such as letterpress, overprinting and magnetic ink, this transparency often drives the end result. Graphic Thought Facility's engraved plastic portraits for the exhibition "Stealing Beauty" neatly summarise the exhibition's premise that unloved, ubiquitous objects can be

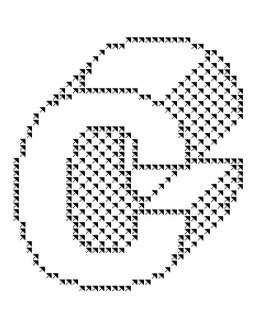

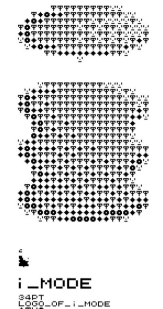

SEX PISTOLS
MINT
FROM ALBUM~NEVER_MIND_BOLLOCKS~/DESIGN BY JAMY REID
MINT

ALAMED
24PT
BITMAP_FONT
A

LINO SCRIF
48PT_REGULAR
OUTLINE FONT(TYPE1)
♥&♡

i_MODE
34PT
LOGO_OF_i_MODE
♦♥♡

COBER PEEDY
12PT
BITMAP_FONT

recontextualised to become something extra-ordinary. Similarly, their treatment for the book Project #26765 – FLIRT, using lenticular panels, fluorescent pink highlighter and spontaneous doodles, signals a love for unsophisticated, less than refined visual languages. The notion of simplicity is integral to this transparency of process; the design is all about observation and editing. But, perversely, richness is to be found in the most simple of solutions.

Humour is another important element. Never taking itself too seriously, much of the work in Specials offers up unexpected and often quirky references. It's a quiet, gentle humour that permeates the work, often providing the key by which to access its meaning. Occasionally, it rises to become something more wicked; see Bump's embroidered tourist badges and half-mast sand castle flags. Undoubtedly there is an intensely personal dimension to the work and for many of these designers, there is no distinction between self-expression and commercial jobs. Pure pleasure in process combines with playful observations of everyday life – whether it be in bantering office culture, nostalgic childhood books, or comic daily routine – to produce a personal interpretation of a brief. A far cry from the blandness of anonymous corporate solutions, these designers stamp their authorship all over this work, making it personal and in the process giving us something with which we can identify.

"We see our designs as objects rather than images on a piece of paper", say Dutch group Experimental Jetset; this speaks volumes about the importance of tactile qualities. In an age when we're all part-time virtual space dwellers, the "real" begins to take on an added resonance. Hence these adventurous investigations into the tactile, combining found

objects, special papers, inks and a multitude of materials such as foil, plastics, wood, and the unapologetic fact that designers are creating graphic design out of "stuff". Ian Wright "draws" portraits by amassing coloured crayons or plastic beads; Jon Hares creates letterforms with furniture; Elektrosmog produce a whole range of products, from embroidered postcards to swimsuits, while åbäke turn graphics into wallpaper, and once made giant letters, which they later sold at the Victoria and Albert Museum's Village Fete.

In compiling Specials we didn't set out simply to celebrate the work of a new generation of designers. Rather, the aim was to capture a current mood that we felt was blind to national borders, as well as age. While many designers featured here are recently-graduated "bright young things", others are more established. What they share is a desire to reclaim a sense of the often overlooked, the strangely beautiful and the gently perverse, as, in effect, an anti-dote to the computer-generated, sensory overload of technological whizzery that has invaded the mainstream media. From acclaimed designers and educators, such as Graphic Thought Facility and Paul Elliman, to up and coming practices, such as Golden Masters in the Netherlands, Happypets Products in Switzerland and the graphics/pop combo Delaware in Japan, this new mood has a foundation in the personal, the playful and the hand-made. And, while an unmitigated over-dependence on digital technology threatens to turn graphic design into a sophisticated yet sterile creative expression, the influence of a more tempered, personal and thought-provoking approach might just save the day.

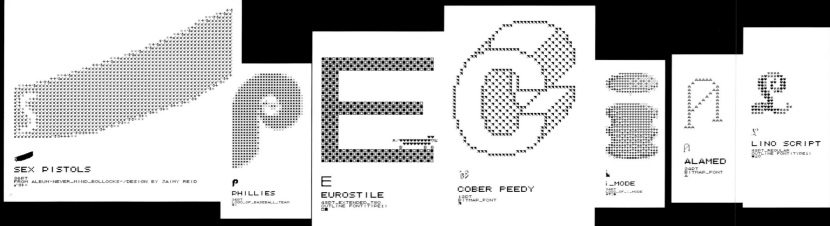

A2-Graphics/SW/HK	info@a2-graphics.co.uk
åbäke	a.b.a.k.e@free.fr
Automatic	automatic@appleonline.net
BCD	contact.bcd@virgin.net
Bettler, Aalex	olaaalex@hotmail.com
Bilak, Peter	peterb@rainside.sk
Blue, Kyle	brotherblue@zerobrothers.com
Bump	bump@btconnect.com
Burrill, Anthony	anthony@friendchip.com
Buxo, Thomas	thomas@buxo.demon.nl
Delaware	samata@pop06.odn.ne.jp
Elektrosmog	iloveyou@esmog.org
Elliman Paul	paul.elliman@yale.edu
Experimental Jetset	experimental@jetset.nl
Fetis, Laurent	l.fetis@noos.fr
Finn, Lizzie	lizzie.finn@virgin.net
Foundation 33	eatock/solhaug@foundation33.com
Goggin, James	james@practise.co.uk
goodwill	goodwill@cable.a2000.nl
Graphic Thought Facility	paul@graphicthoughtfacility.com
Green, Robert	rob@fgjs.demon.co.uk
Happypets Products	happypetsproducts@hotmail.com
Hares, Jon	jonhares@btinternet.com
Hyperkit	tim@hyperkit.co.uk

P
PHILLIES
36DT
LOGO_OF_BASEBALL_TEAM

E
EUROSTILE
48DT_EXTENDED_TWO
OUTLINE FONT(TYPE1)

O
OCRA
12PT_REGULAR
OUTLINE FONT(TYPE1)

P
PHILLIES
36DT
LOGO_OF_BASEBALL_TEAM

LINO SCRIPT
48DT_REGULAR
OUTLINE FONT(TYPE1)

E
EUROSTILE
48DT_EXTENDED_TWO
OUTLINE FONT(TYPE1)

Kerr Noble	info@kerrnoble.com
Kiock, Valerie	valerie.kiock@williamsandphoa.co.uk
Kurz, Carolin	ckurzuk@aol.com
Lust	lust@lust.nl
Mahoney, Robbie	robbie.mahoney@virgin.net
Molecule	molecule@dds.nl
Morgan, John	john@bookdesign.co.uk
NB Studio	b.stott@nbstudio.co.uk
Office of CC	ver@xs4all.nl
Ohio Girl	andy@ohiogirl.com
Golden Masters	hl@ok-ams.nl
OPX	bill@opx.co.uk
reala	lrnt@reala.org
Reinfurt, David O R G	david@o-r-g.com
Revell, David	david.r@tangodesign.com
Rich, Alex	thank.you@virgin.net
Sans + Baum	sans@dircon.co.uk
Sansbury, Ben	ben@aggressivepeace.com
Secondary Modern	secmo@dircon.co.uk
Unit	donna@unitdesign.co.uk
Wehrspahn, Niels	niels@copy.li
Woodtli, Martin	martinwoodtli@datacomm.ch
Wright, Ian	mail@mrianwright.co.uk

end

Première of touring video exhibition
19 May 7.00 - 8.00pm Royal College of Art
RCAfé 2nd floor Darwin Building

Running Order: Dominique Vezina **Trucks 02:44** Otto Berchem **Hand Catching Spanish Sausage 03:36** Luis Felipe Ortega & Daniel Guzmán **06:30** John Strutton **Father, Son & Scary Ghost: Scary Spider 00:30** A.P. Komen & Karen Murphy **The Secret Garden 05:00** John Strutton **Smack ma boy up.... tenderly 03:15** Tove Lamm **Meantime 03:15** It looks like rain... has been curated by nn12

A2-Graphics/SW/HK
"It looks like rain" travelling exhibition promo poster
Royal College of Art/Visual Arts Administration
May 1999, UK
The poster is composed of 58,560 raindrops.

Face Painting 02:25 Georgina Starr **Cat Conversation from A Visit to a Small Planet 05:00** John Strutton **Father, Son & Scary Ghost: Mad Dog 00:30** Matt Hale **A bit of slap and tickle**
& Scary Ghost: The Worm 00:30 Maurice O'Connell **level 28 10:00** André van Bergen **Untitled 03:40** Luis Felipe Ortega & Daniel Guzmán **REMAKE: Fountain 00:28** Kevin Francis Gray

SPENT.

HOMEBASE
LONDON, BATTERSEA
Tel No. 0171 228 7666
Vat No. 638 5287 04

04/10/99   TRANS:6044   TILL:041
18:37   CASHIER:9017 STORE:P667

FIRE EXTING (R)
5099383040320   7.99

T O T A L   7.99

CASH   10.00
CHANGE   2.01

VAT AT 17.5% (R)   1.19
        TOTAL TAX   1.19

        You're better OFF At
           HOMEBASE
Why not apply for a SPEND & SAVE card?
The more you spend, the more you save.

Fire extinguisher
1999
Dry powder fire
extinguisher,
screws

A2-Graphics/SW/HK

"Spent" catalogue for one-day exhibition
Commissioned by curator Emma Mahony
November 1999, UK

Twenty-one artists each received a £10 postal order to spend on the
execution of an artwork. The catalogue was produced with the aid of
a photocopier; A3 black and white photocopies were simply folded in
half, collated and stapled together.

46 bittersweet

A2-Graphics/SW/HK
The Interactive Colouring Book
Nov 2000, UK
A digital interpretation of "painting by numbers". Using an on-screen
display as opposed to the traditional printed page, the user is able
to digitally paint, erase and repaint, over and over again.

David Reinfurt, ORG Inc.
Brills Content poster walls
Brills Content magazine/Ogilvy and Mather Inc.
March 2000, USA

Three poster wall locations in New York publicise the redesign of Brills Content. At each site six-feet-tall letters appear in alphabetical order over the course of a month, so as to reveal the campaign message. Follow the progression through this book. Photography: Vicky Samburnaris.

Bump
"Doodul"
2001, UK
Viral poster campaign for eyestorm.com using a digital-effect
typeface that may be customised to create random words.
Photographs by Matt Higgs.

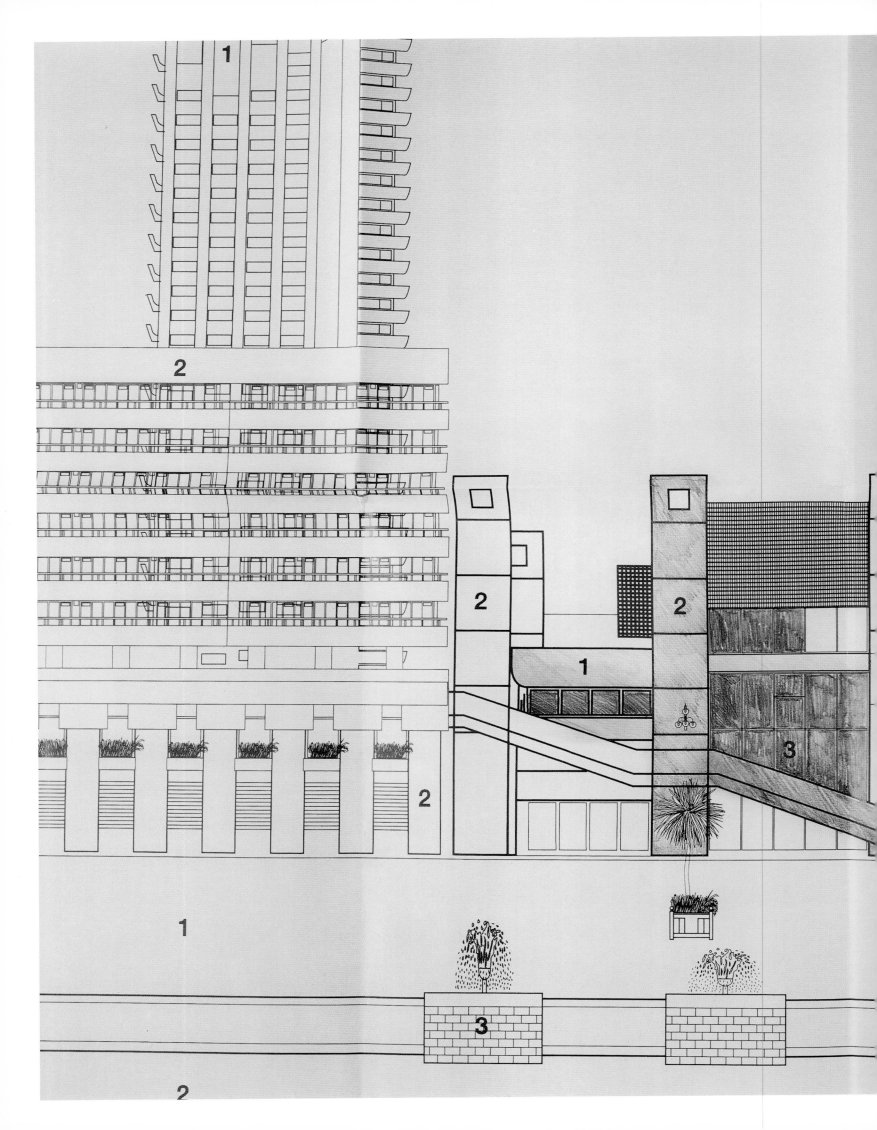

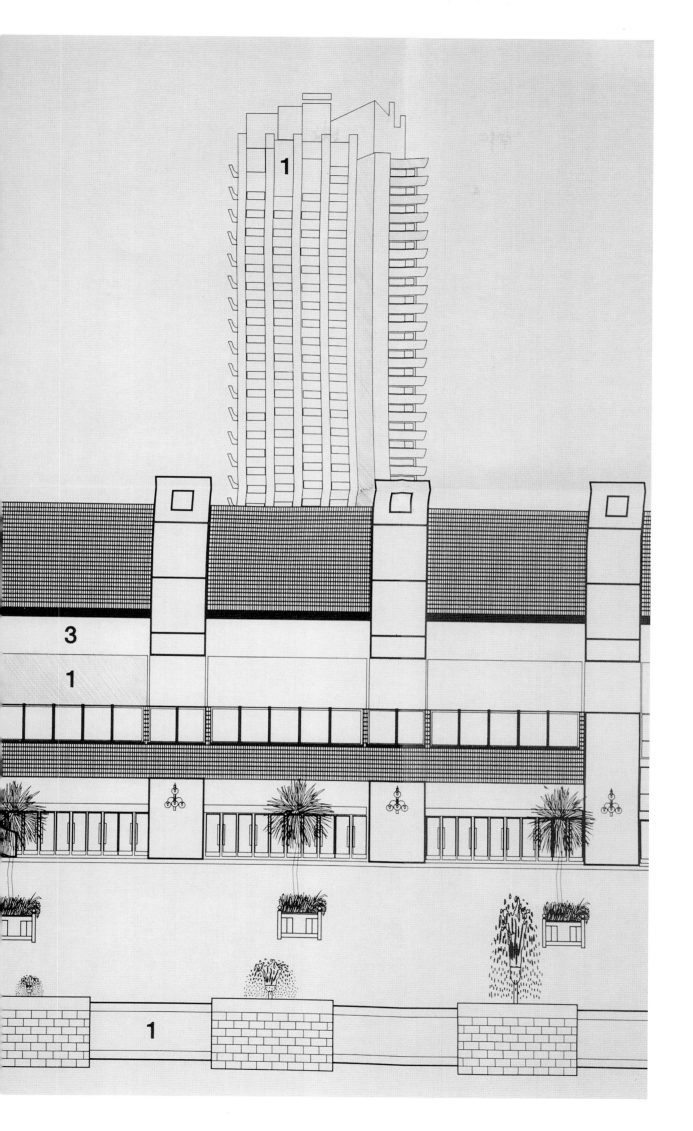

Bump
"Grey Matters Colouring Kit"
2001, UK

A colour-by-numbers pack with an unusually urban subject matter; contains 2H, HB and 3B pencils for colouring-in concrete resulting in an instant D-I-Y artwork.

BARBICAN CENTRE

GREY MATTERS COLOURING KIT

COLOUR BY NUMBERS. includes 1x 2H 1x HB and 1x 3B pencil for concrete colouring   COPYRIGHT BUMP 2001

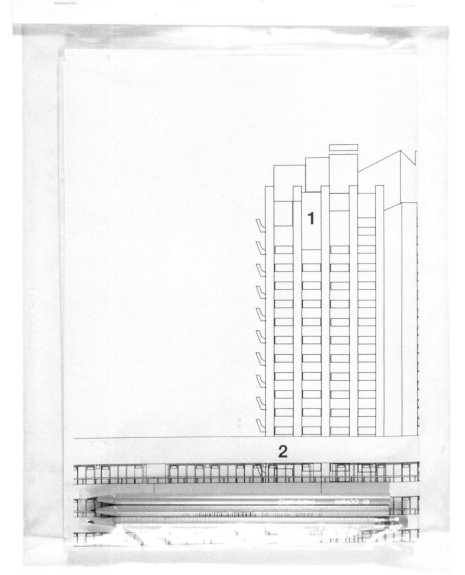

TOURIST TRAP

EMBROIDERED BADGE

one colour version   COPYRIGHT BUMP 2001

HALF-MAST

SANDCASTLE FLAGS

COLOUR VERSION   COPYRIGHT BUMP 2001

HALF-MAST

SANDCASTLE FLAGS

BLACK AND WHITE VERSION   COPYRIGHT BUMP 2001

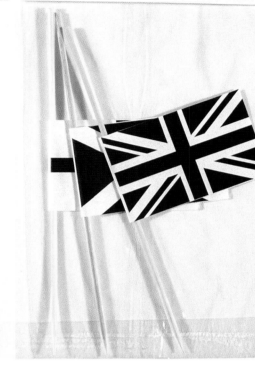

Bump
"Half-mast Sandcastle Flags"
2001, UK
Every man's home is a sand castle.

Bump
"Back seat driver"
2001, UK
Audio cassette to keep you company on Britain's highways and byways.

Bump
"Tourist Trap"
2001, UK
Embroidered sew-on badge

Bump
"Grey Matters Colouring Kit"
2001, UK

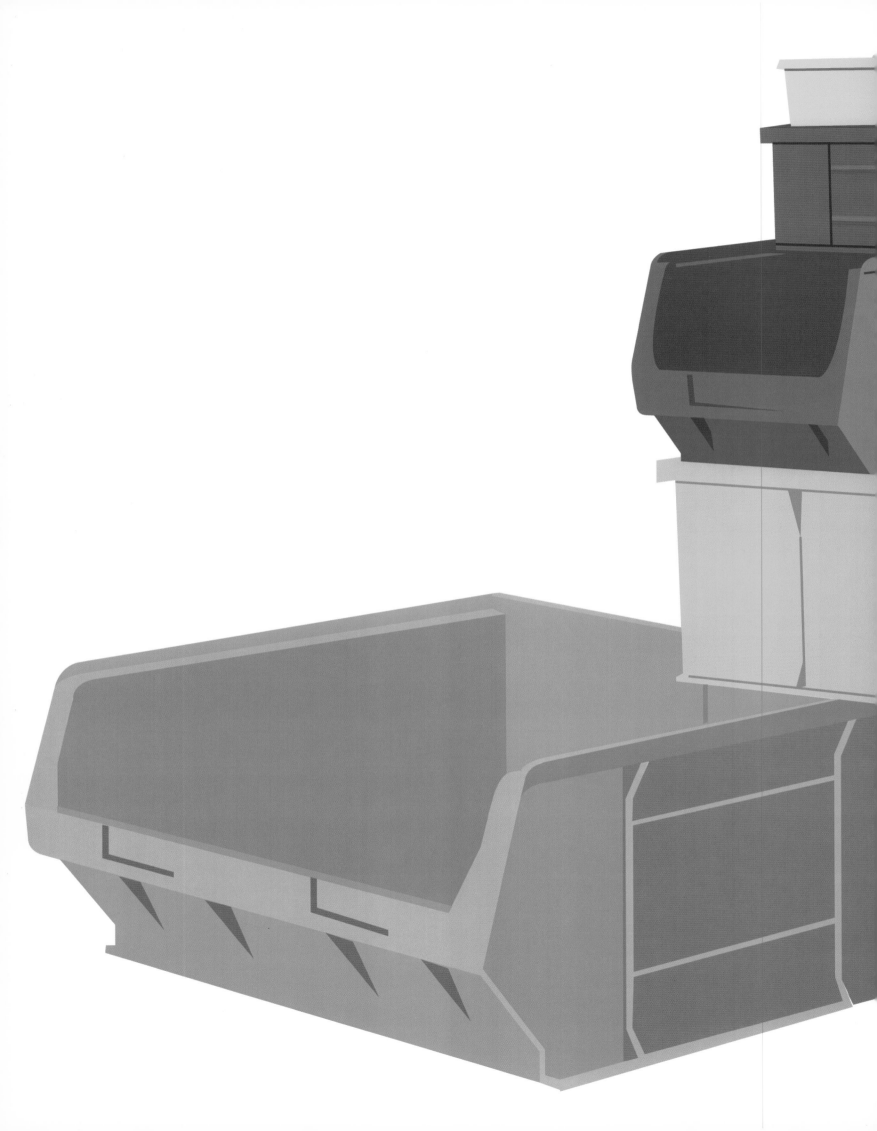

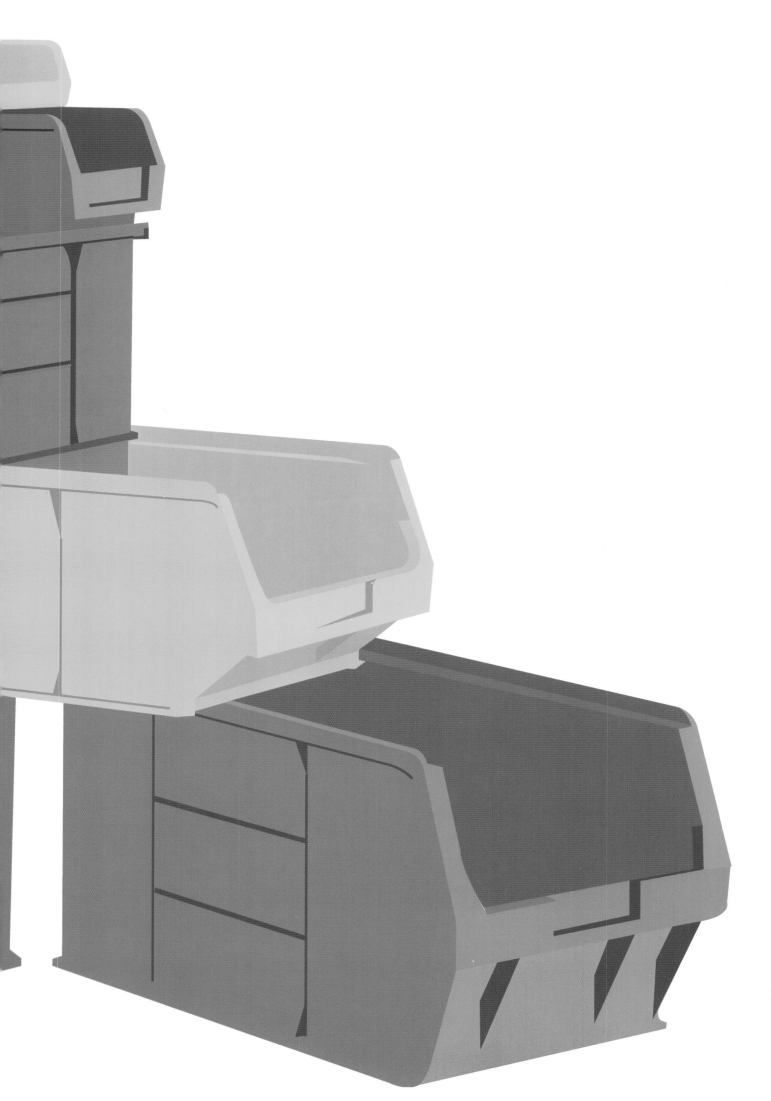

James Goggin/Practise
Moving card
January 2001, UK

James Goggin/Practise
Office World
1999/2000, UK
From a project about colour, these photos illustrate unexpected occurrences of colour within intentionally uniform and banal setting – offices, stationery superstores and factories – places that represent the concept of "work".

James Goggin/Practise
Happy Light
Photograph
2000, Switzerland
A found object, a piece of anthropomorphic vandalism, could serve as a prototype for improving street lighting, so as to make urban areas happier places to be after dark.

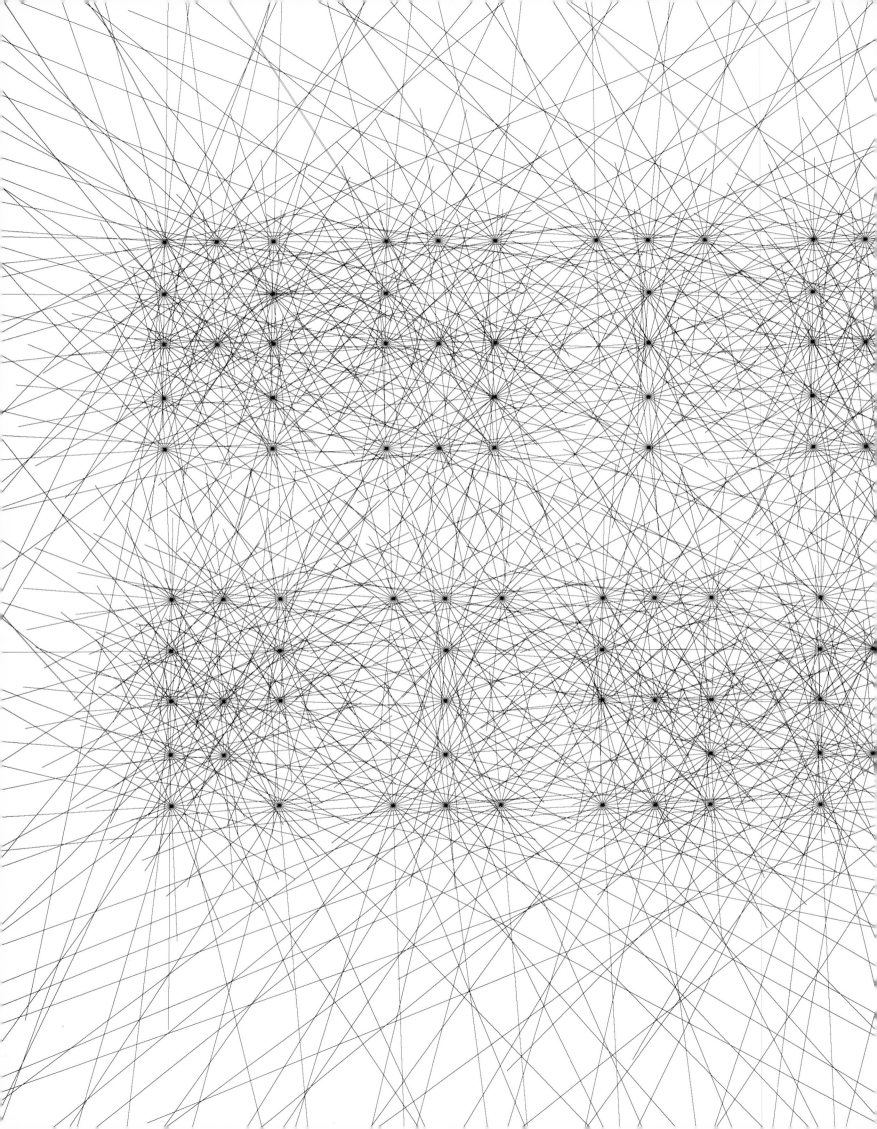

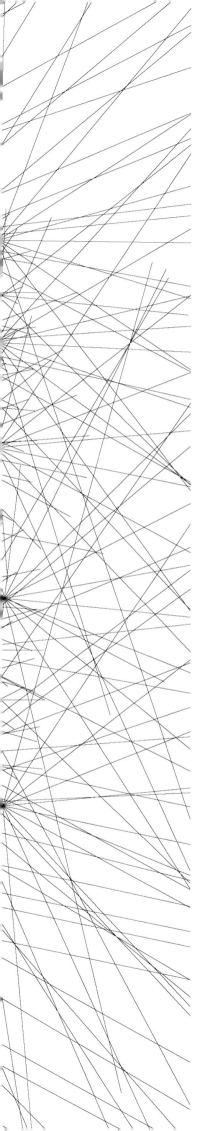

James Goggin/Practise
Asterix Matrix font
2000/2001, UK

A prototype font conceived as a networked system, with each letter and
word having a visible connection with another so that the more that is
written, the more intricate (and less legible) the text becomes. Sentences
are hidden in the mass of asterisks, with letters discernible because of the
nuclei of the stars that make up the 3x5 dot matrix.

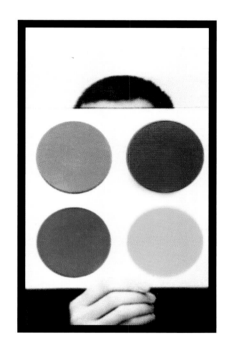

James Goggin
Business card
2000, UK

Een multi-disciplinair remix spektakel ✳ Aanvang: 20:00 uur ✳ Entree: 17,50 gulden ✳ Presentatie: Kees Brienen en Nadja Hüpscher ✳
Voorverkoop alleen bij AUB en Postkantoren ✳ Voor BNO-leden: entree: 12,50 gulden (wel reserveren op nummer: 020 624 47 48) ✳
Aansluitend in de grote zaal: AUDIO ✳ Jack gaat door in de bovenzaal... ✳ Meer info: www.jackprojects.nl of www.paradiso.nl

POPKIT

Met o.a.:
Ontwerpers/ kunstenaars:
Electrosmog & Ping Pong
EGBG
studenten Rietveld Academie
studenten Sandberginstituut
Maurice Scheltens
Devon Ress
Raf Snippe
Jacob de Baan
Pieter Verweij
Marcus Oakley
Margit Lukacs
Annelies Vanoyken
Erik Weeda
Arnout Kilian
Maartje Fliervoet

Financiële ondersteuning:
Fonds voor Beeldende Kunsten, Vormgeving en Bouwkunst.
Materiaalfonds voor Beeldende Kunst en Vormgeving.

paradiso
ur ijdag
25 mei

jack o4
popkit
ou den
smaster.

jack o4

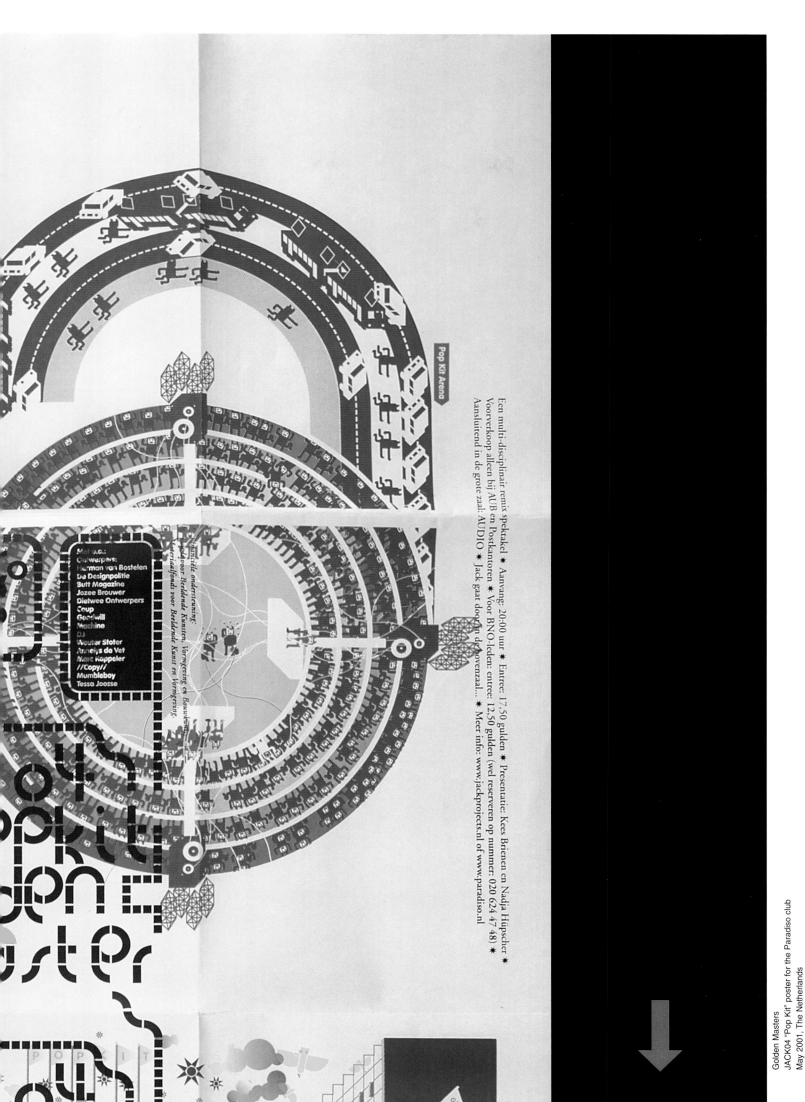

Golden Masters
JACK04 "Pop Kit" poster for the Paradiso club
May 2001, The Netherlands

Een multi-disciplinair remix spektakel ∗ Aanvang: 20:00 uur ∗ Entree: 17,50 gulden ∗ Presentatie: Kees Brienen en Nadja Hüpscher ∗ Voorverkoop alleen bij AUB en Postkantoren ∗ Voor BNO-leden: entree: 12,50 gulden (wel reserveren op nummer: 020 624 47 48) ∗ Aansluitend in de grote zaal: AUDIO ∗ Jack gaat door in de bovenzaal... ∗ Meer info: www.jackprojects.nl of www.paradiso.nl

Financiële ondersteuning:
Fonds voor Beeldende Kunsten, Vormgeving en Bouwkunst.
Materiaalfonds voor Beeldende Kunst en Vormgeving

gol den smaster

Jack oy popkit ol den smaster

par ad iso vr ijdag 25 mei

Met o.a.:
Schrijvers:
Maria Barnas
Astrid Lampe
Noortje Marres
Ruben van Gogh
Arjan Witte
Tommy Wieringa
Jan Rothuizen

Architekten:
Sub Office Architekten

Met o.a.:
Muzikanten:
KODI
50.000.000 Evis Fans
Shaemus
Sputnik
Pfaff
sal
Damer
de PJ Roggeband
DJ Radar
John Wayne Shot Me
Pers I

Financiële ondersteuning:
Fonds voor Beeldende Kunst...
Materiaalfonds voor Beelden...

Een m...
Voorv...
Aansl...

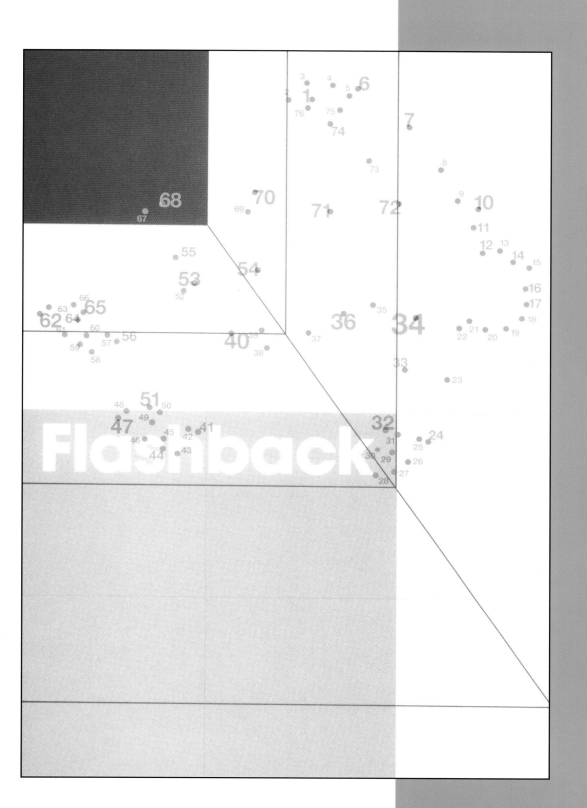

Golden Masters
"Call me, OK?" business card
Spring 1999, The Netherlands
OK changed their name to Golden Masters in 2001

Golden Masters
"Pop Kit" CD cover for the Howtoplays
Howtoplays/JACK
April 2001., The Netherlands

Golden Masters
"Flashback"
Het Veem Theatre, Amsterdam
January 2000, The Netherlands

Lizzie Finn
"Things to make and do" album sleeve for Moloko
The Echo Label
April 2000, UK/Japan
The band wanted something totally unlike a typically minimalist
dance-music sleeve. The title came after seeing the design.

Lizzie Finn
"Indigo" Moloko CD cover
The Echo Label
November 2000, UK/Japan

leaving ... and stuffing. ...
turning and stuffing. ...
corners, turn to right side ...
right side, turn under 6mm all around
nose circle and baste. Baste the felt
nose circle into the opening, easing it.
Stitch with running stitches about 3mm
from edge to form a realistic snout ridge.
Stuff nose out of shape; it should look flat
from the front. Stitch across opening.

Cheeks
Glue each brown nostril and pink cheek
piece into position as shown and oversew
all around each piece. Cut 2 lengths of
blue yarn and glue ends to cheeks.

The time is now
05:20
You're my last breath. You're a breath of
fresh air to me. Hi, I'm empty. Tell me
you care for me. You're the first thing.
And the last thing on my mind. In your
arms I feel. Sunshine. On a promise. A
day dream yet to come. Time is upon us,
Oh but the night is young.
Flowers blossom. In the winter time. In
your arms I feel.

Sunshine
Give up yourself unto the moment
The time is now
Give up yourself unto the moment
Let's make this moment last

You may find yourself. Out on a limb for
me. Could you except it as. A part of your
destiny? I give all I have. But it's not
enough. And my patience is shot.
So I'm calling your bluff.
Give up yourself unto the moment.
The time is now. Give up yourself unto
the moment. Let's make this moment,
last.
And we gave it time. All eyes are on the
clock. But time takes too much time
Please make the waiting stop. And the
atmosphere is charged. In you I trust.
I feel no fear as I. Do as I must.
Give up yourself unto the moment.
The time is now. Give up yourself unto
the moment. Let's make this moment,
last.
Tempted by fate. But I won't hesitate The
time is now. And I can't wait. I've been
empty too long. Took a chance and now
it's gone. And the time has come And the
night is young. The time is now. Let's
make this moment last.
Give up yourself unto the moment.
The time is now. Give up yourself unto
the moment. Let's make this moment,
last.

50

Change my face. But it won't erase, I Changed my
heart. When my soul changed hands. What if, when I
find myself? Made new plans. I don't really like myself?
Underhand. What if when I look inside? Change my
name. I don't like much what I find? But I remain the
same. *Change my name I remain the same. Change my
name I remain the same. Try again, another new
beginning.* Change my course. But I can't change my
ways D I V O R C E. Will you count the days. What if,
when I find myself? Change my tune. I don't really like
myself? But I stand on shifting stand. What if when I
look inside? When I change my nameMy heart was
changing hands. Baby you'll never understand
    Change my name I remain the same. Change my
name I remain the same. Try again, another new
beginning. If I, if I could just. Slip from the net. Try to
forget. I hang my head. In regret. If I, if, If I could just
But it's too much. Slip from my skin. I try again. Another
new beginning.
    Change my name I remain the same. Change my
name I remain the same. Try again, another new
beginning. Change my name I remain the same......
I remain the same. I remain the same. I remain the same

Leave open
for stuffing

24

Eyes
Cut 13 or 14 length...
18mm long, and glu...
of the felt eyelid an...
D to D as shown ...
of felt strip sli... dow...
st... alon... n eyelashes to shape.

... line of glue along the ...
... ar, and glue to top of head ...
...tion matching F, G with K, J.

Dumb Inc.
04:27 Oh Yeah...Yeah Oh Yeah. Dumb
dumb. So sweet so young. You're not
supposed to swallow. Your bubble gum.

Chicken foot
dim sum
Knuckle head. Knuckle head
Look what you've done

Dumb
dumbing it down. Take a look around.
You and me are free to be the. Dumbest in
town. Young gun. Excuse the pun.
The pandemonium has. Just begun.
Dumb dumb. We're dumbing it down.
Got a head full. Of cotton wool. But life
for me. Is never dull. To fulfil. You have
to fill full. I turned around and. Bought a
round and. poured another one. proud
fool. you're just too cool for school. full
moon come soon. and when the moon is
not quite round. where can the missing bit
be found. be proud to be profound.

Dumb dumb. We're dumbing it down.
Devoid. We are malcontent. We're not
entirely sure. Of our intent. Brain washed
we suffer. Memory loss. Ho hum play
dumb come. Little boy lost. The time
bomb. Is ticking. Quickening, quickening
Quickening, quickening. Quickening...

Dumb dumb. We're dumbing it down
Dumb Dumb...

I feel like. A drop in the ocean. Just a ripple. On expanding
seas. If the shoe fits. I swear it. I will wear it. By this shin-
ing stiletto. I do decree. I'm half full and my glass is empty
say so long and wave goodbye. I've been searching. For new
ways. To get lost. There's got to be someplace, Somewhere I'll
never be found. I can fend for myself. Could pretend to
myself. I will play the wild rover. Though my horse may be
blind. I'm half full and. My glass is empty. say so long and
wave goodbye. all the binds that tie are. there for a reason
you won't fond the prairie. it's folly to try. **(01:58)**

43

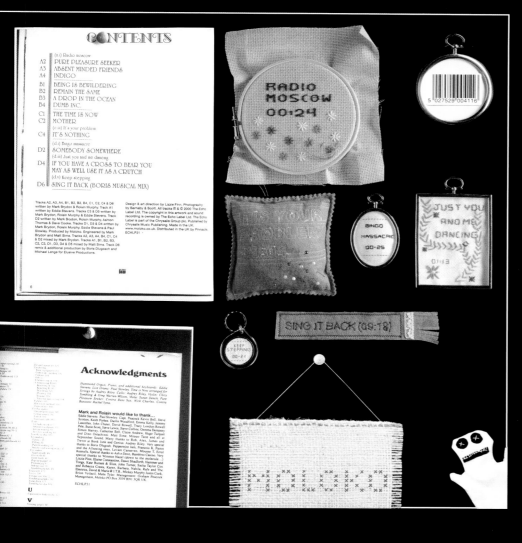

Lizzie Finn
"Things to make and do" album sleeve for Moloko
The Echo Label
November 2000, UK/Japan

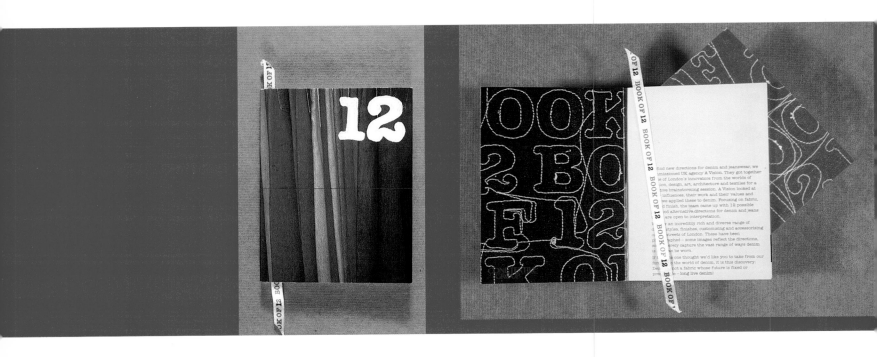

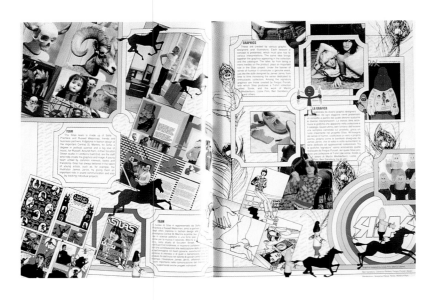

Lizzie Finn
Book of 12
Summer 2000
Cone Textiles Group
2000, UK
One of a series of books commissioned by a textiles company with each edition produced and published in a different city. This one was published by A Vision in London and feautures photography by Jason Evans.

Lizzie Finn
Silas catalogue Autumn/Winter 1999/2000
Silas and Maria
2000, UK
A "medieval photostory" was inspired by girls' annuals from the 1970s and 1980s.

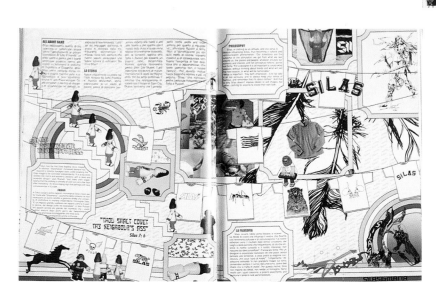

Lizzie Finn
Silas special feature in Sport and Street Collezione magazine
Spring 2001, Italy

Hyperkit:
35 Kingsland Road
London E2 8AA
Tel 020 7684 1500
www.hyperkit.co.uk
info@hyperkit.co.uk

HYPERKIT IS A LONDON
BASED MULTI-DISCIPLINED
DESIGN TEAM FORMED IN
2001 BY KATE SCLATER
AND TIM BALAAM //
DESIGN // GRAPHIC / WEB /
INTERACTIVE / 3D / EXHIBITION

EMAIL TIM

TIM BALAAM GRADUATED FROM
MA COMMUNICATION STUDIES
AT THE RCA IN SUMMER 2000
AND SUBSEQUENTLY WORKED
FREELANCE AT OKUPL

EMAIL KATE

KATE SCLATER GRADUATED
FROM BA GRAPHIC DESIGN AT
CAMBERWELL IN 1999 AND
WORKED AS A DESIGNER AT
AMX ON FROM THEN UNTIL 2001.

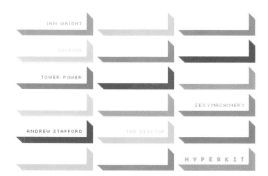

IAN WRIGHT

DELIRIUM

TOWER POWER

SEXYMACHINERY

ANDREW STAFFORD   THE DESKTOP

HYPERKIT

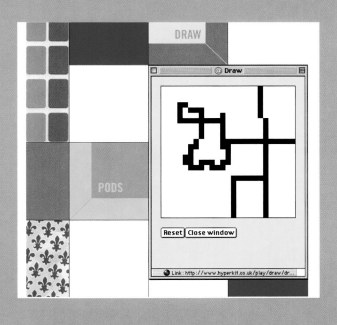

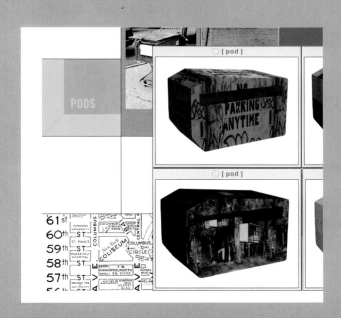

Hyperkit
Website for Hyperkit: www.hyperkit.co.uk
2001, UK

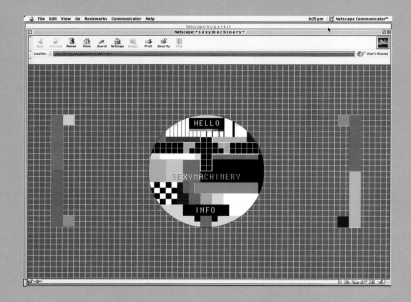

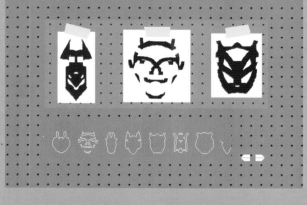

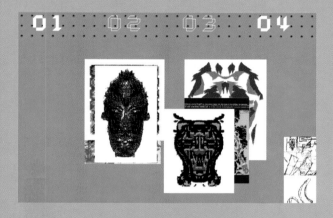

Hyperkit
Holding page for sexymachinery website
2001, UK

Hyperkit
Website for illustrator Ian Wright: www.mrianwright.co.uk
2001, UK

Frith Kerr, Amelia Noble and Ian Wright
"Seaside Suicide" poster campaign and badges
May 2001, France
Stencil to promote a gig in Cannes by Tony Kaye's band "K".
May 2001, France

Frith Kerr, Amelia Noble and Ian Wright
"Seaside Suicide" stencil for poster campaign
May 2001, France

LE JEUDI 17 MAI 2001

DE 21 HEURES À 2 HEURES DU MATIN

MAN RAY CLUB

LA PLAGE MAN RAY/L'VASION

BOULEVARD LA CROISETTE

FACE MIRAMAR–CANNES

K

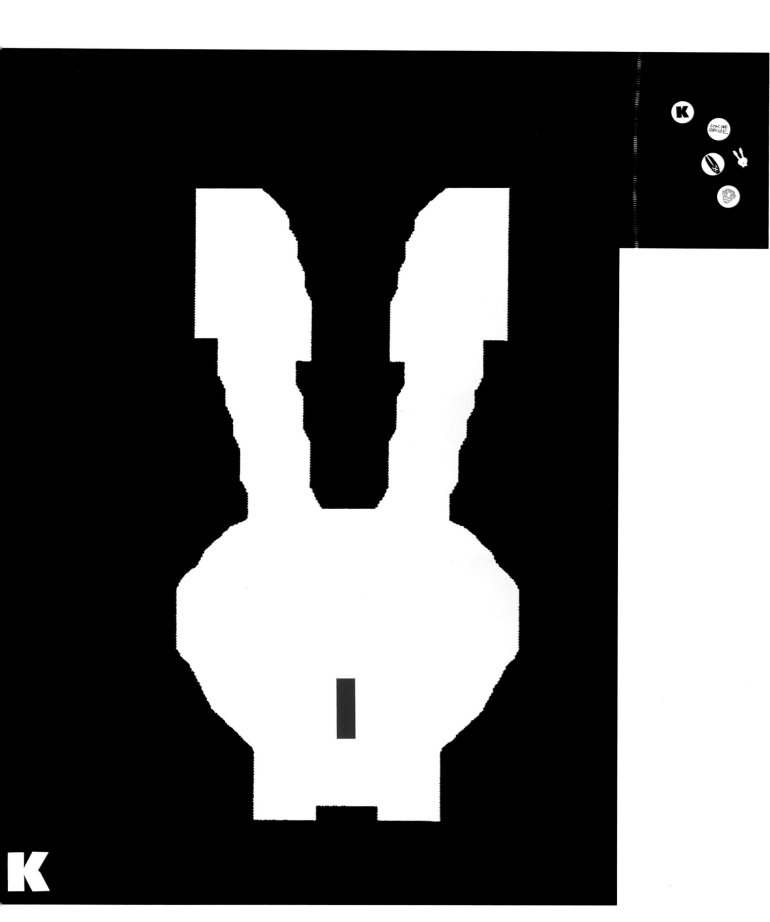

Ian Wright
"Seaside Suicide" poster campaign and badges
May 2001, France

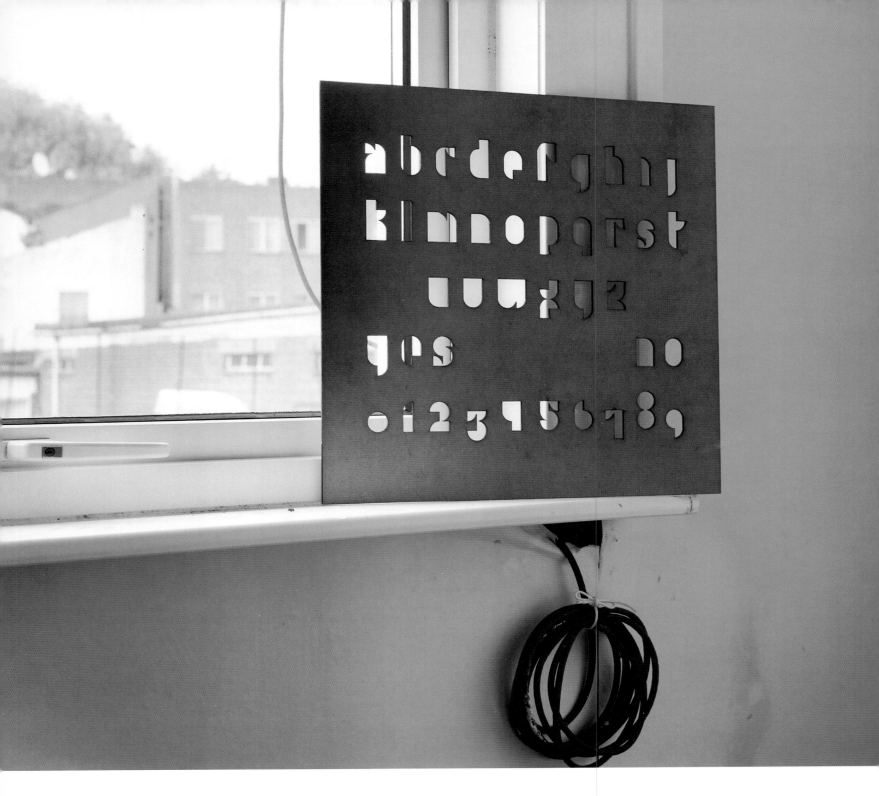

Paul Elliman
Ouija Board stencil
2001, USA

A remake of a stencil cut in glass by Josef Albers in 1926. Elliman,
who teaches at Yale University's design school, which was set up
by Albers in 1951, has added the words "yes" and "no" making a
ouija board with which to contact Albers and his wife Annie.
With thanks to Nigel Shafran.

NAOMI KLEIN
2/24 2001

NEAL GABLER
2/25 2001

ANDREA CODRINGTON/
PETER HALL/
JULIE LASKY/
MARTY NEUMEIER/
MARTIN C.PEDERSEN/
VéRONIQUE VIENNE
2/24 2001

AIGA STAFF:
RICHARD GREFé
DEBORAH ALDRICH
PAMELA AVILES
KELLEY BEAUDOIN
MOLLY BEVERSTEIN
2/25 2001
NEXT PAGE →

STEVEN JOHNSON
2/24 2001

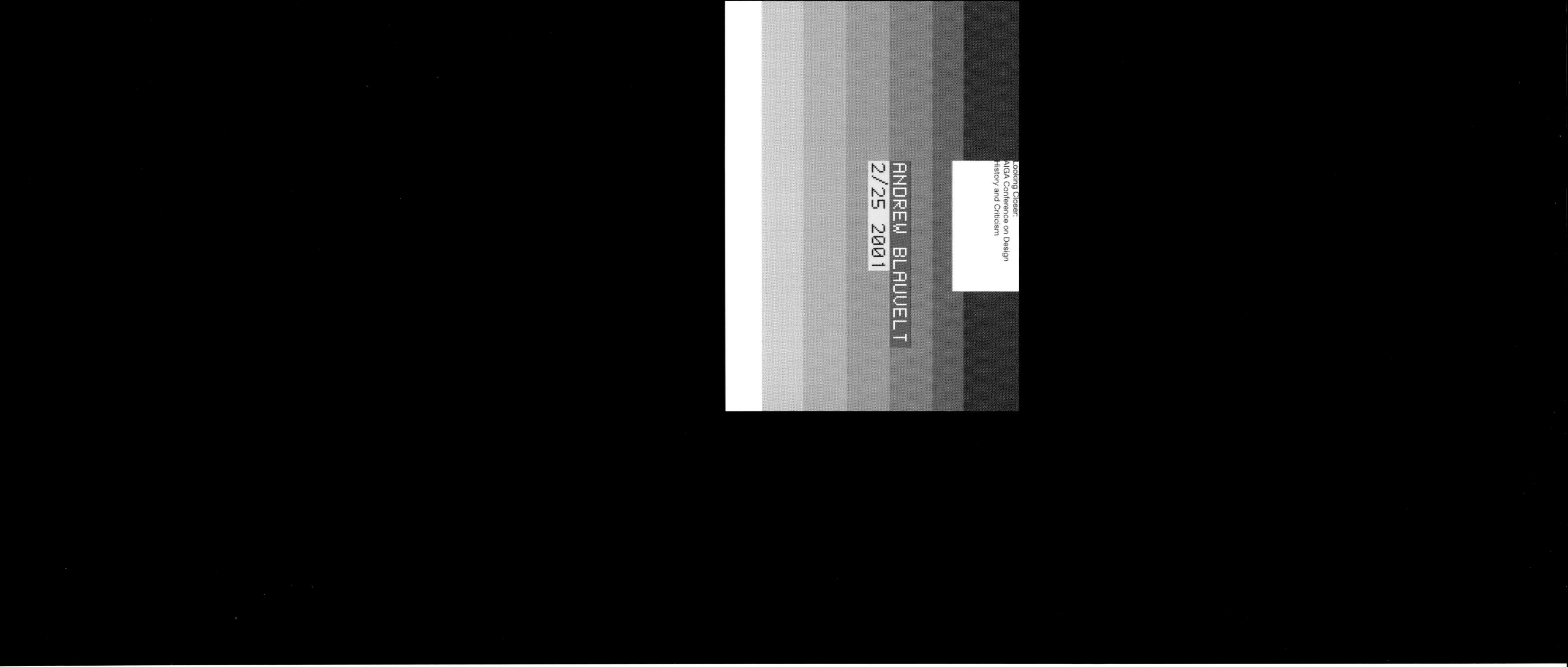

Looking Closer:
AIGA Conference on Design
History and Criticism

ANDREW BLAUVELT
2/25 2001

Paul Elliman
Poster and conference titles for AIGA conference "Looking Closer"
American Institute of Graphic Arts
2001, USA
These conference titles are based on projector tests. Elliman's work refers to ideas about communicating via technologies across various distances. The poster was produced with assistance from Xerox.

Thanks to Anthony DeVito at Xerox Imaging Standards and David Reinfurt (ORG) at Time + Temperature.

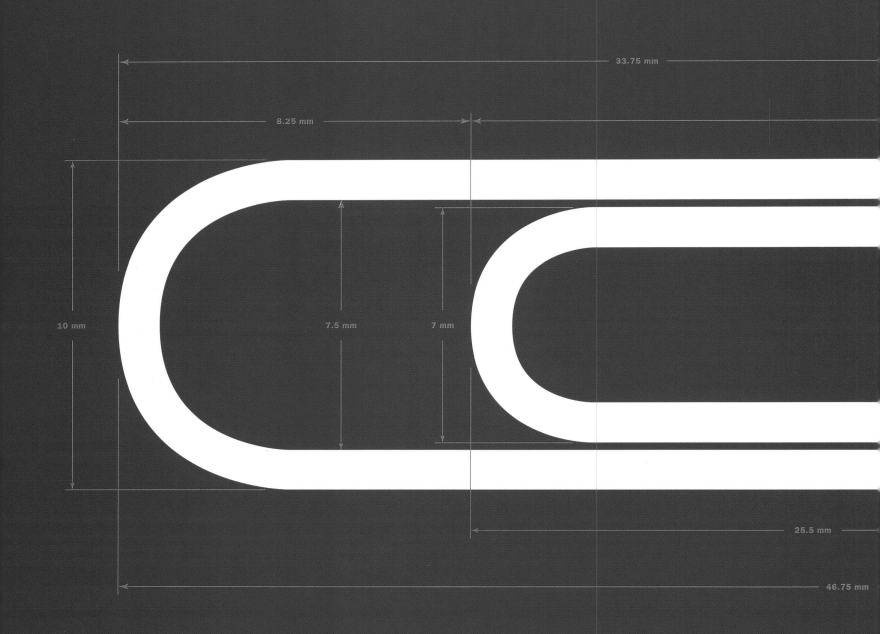

33.75 mm

8.25 mm

10 mm

7.5 mm

7 mm

25.5 mm

46.75 mm

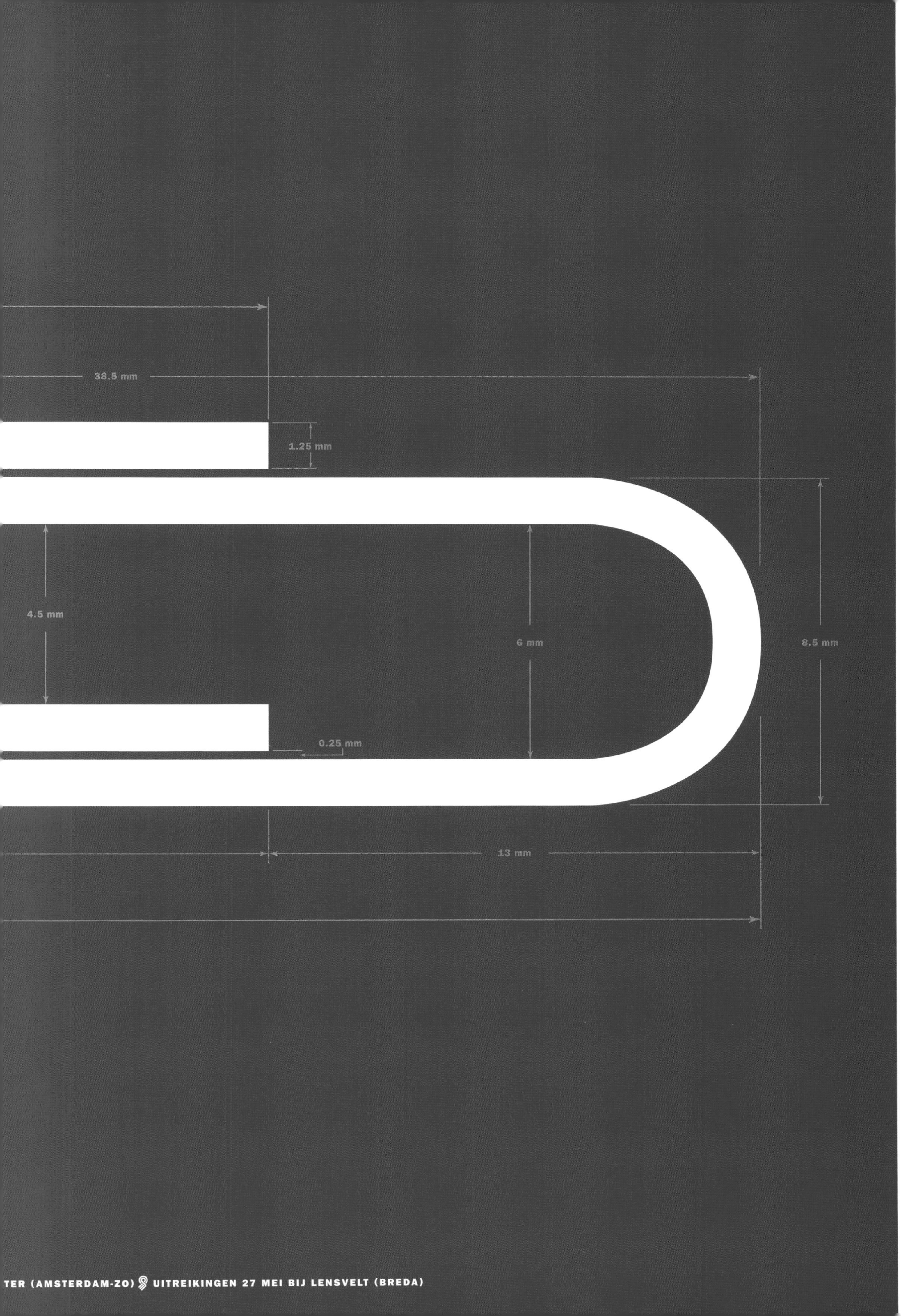

38.5 mm

1.25 mm

4.5 mm

6 mm

8.5 mm

0.25 mm

13 mm

TER (AMSTERDAM-ZO) 𝄞 UITREIKINGEN 27 MEI BIJ LENSVELT (BREDA)

Office of CC
Paper Clip poster
Goed Industrieel Ontwerp
January 1999, The Netherlands

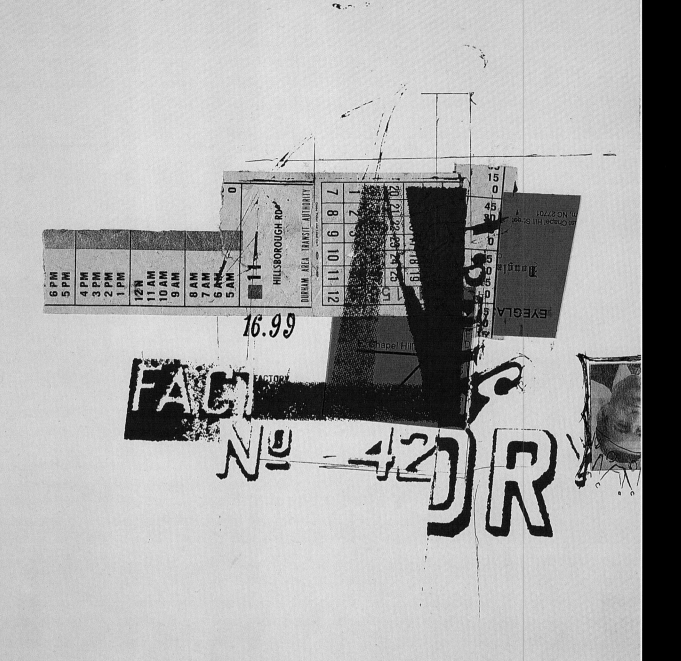

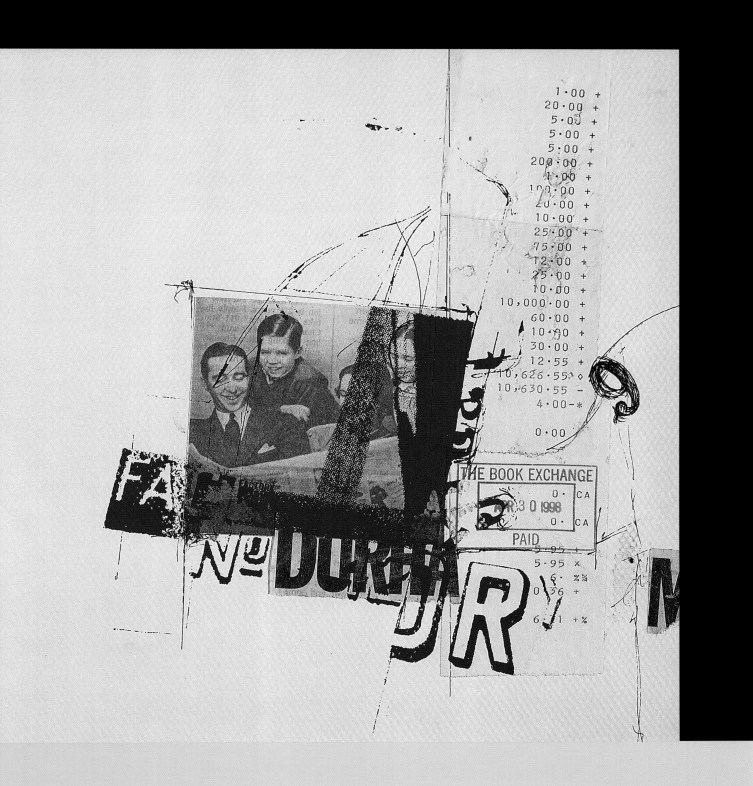

Kyle Blue
Durham
Environmental type exploration
May 1998, USA

Kyle Blue
Durham
Environmental type exploration
May 1998, USA

date/created

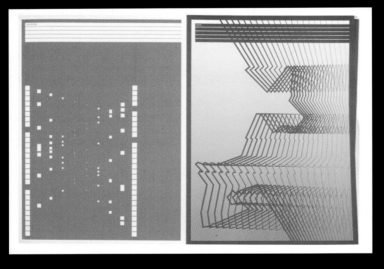

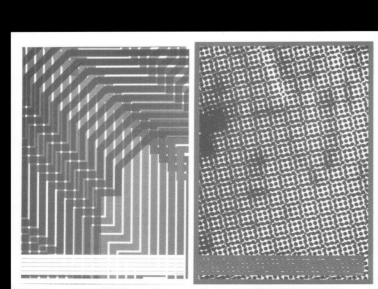

date/created

OPX
Content #1, "Date/Created"
October 2000, UK
Created by Stephen Wells, the first issue of Content took as its
subject a workshop that was held at the Royal Institute of British
Architects on the theme of creativity. Over-printing and various
optical effects were used to highlight the theme.

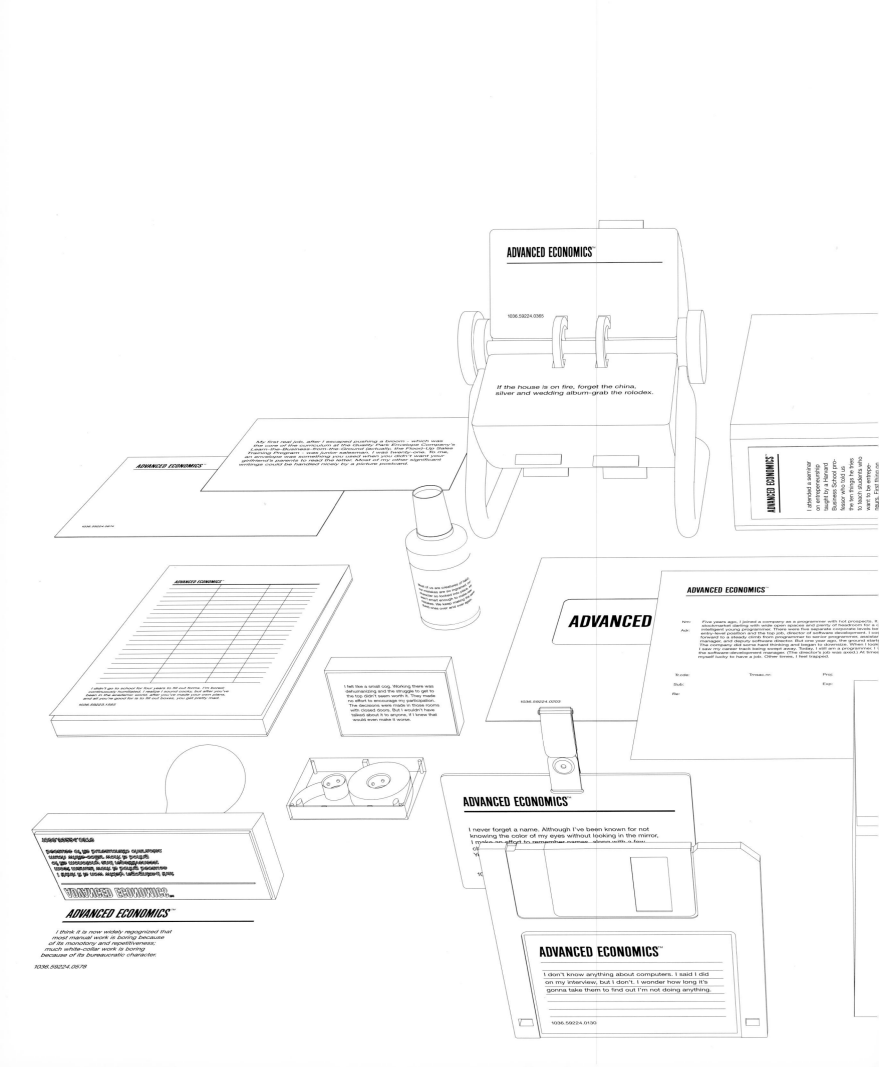

ADVANCED ECONOMICS™

1036.59224.0365

If the house is on fire, forget the china, silver and wedding album-grab the rolodex.

ADVANCED ECONOMICS™

My first real job, after I escaped pushing a broom - which was the core of the curriculum at the Quality Park Envelope Company's Learn-the-Business-from-the-Ground (actually, the Flood)-Up Sales Training Program - was junior salesman. I was twenty-one. To me, an envelope was something you used when you didn't want your girlfriend's parents to read the letter. Most of my other significant writings could be handled nicely by a picture postcard.

1036.59224.0674

ADVANCED ECONOMICS™

I attended a seminar on entrepenurship taught by a Harvard Business School professor who told us the ten things he tries to teach students who want to be entrepeneurs. First thing on...

ADVANCED ECONOMICS™

I didn't go to school for four years to fill out forms. I'm bored, continuously humiliated. I realize I sound cocky, but after you've been in the academic world, after you've made your own plans, and all you're good for is to fill out boxes, you get pretty mad.

1036.59223.1565

Most of us are creatures of habit. ... our mistakes are so ingrained, our character so locked into place ... aren't smart enough to make ... mistakes. We keep making the same ... ones over and over again.

I felt like a small cog. Working there was dehumanizing and the struggle to get to the top didn't seem worth it. They made no effort to encourage my participation. The decisions were made in those rooms with closed doors. But I wouldn't have talked about it to anyone, if I knew that would even make it worse.

ADVANCED ECONOMICS™

ADVANCED

Nm: Five years ago, I joined a company as a programmer with hot prospects. It...
stockmarket darling with wide open spaces and plenty of headroom for a ...
intelligent young programmer. There were five separate corporate levels be...
Adr: entry-level position and the top job, director of software development. I co...
forward to a steady climb from programmer to senior programmer, assistan...
manager, and deputy software director. But one year ago, the ground start...
The company did some hard thinking and began to downsize. When I look...
I saw my career track being swept away. Today, I still am a programmer. I...
the software-development manager. (The director's job was axed.) At time...
myself lucky to have a job. Other times, I feel trapped.

Tr.cde: Trnsac.nr: Proj:

Sub: Exp:

Re:

1036.59224.0203

ADVANCED ECONOMICS™

I think it is now widely recognized that most manual work is boring because of its monotony and repetitiveness; much white-collar work is boring because of its bureaucratic character.

1036.59224.0578

ADVANCED ECONOMICS™

I never forget a name. Although I've been known for not knowing the color of my eyes without looking in the mirror, I make an effort to remember names, along with a few ch...
Y...

ADVANCED ECONOMICS™

I don't know anything about computers. I said I did on my interview, but I don't. I wonder how long it's gonna take them to find out I'm not doing anything.

1036.59224.0130

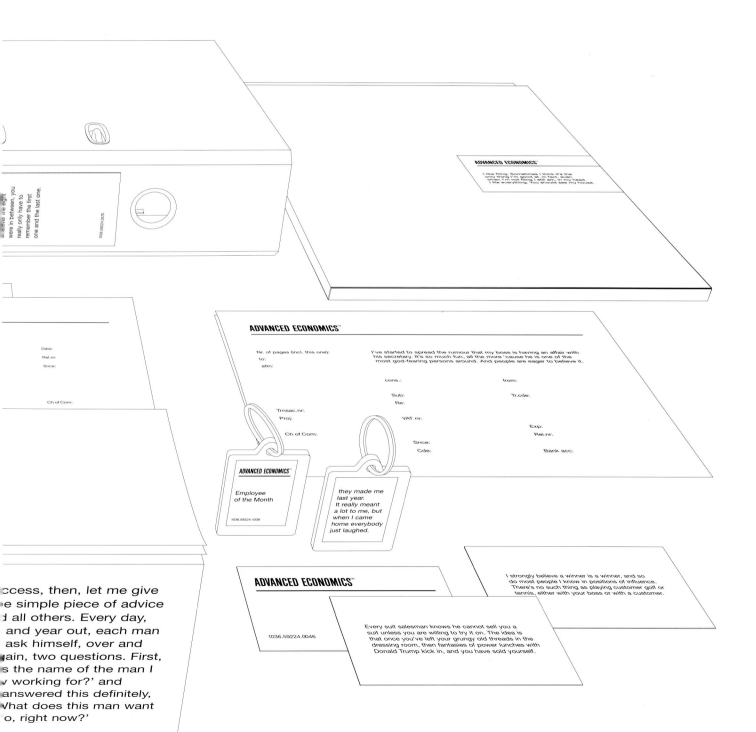

whatever the eight
were in between, you
really only have to
remember the first
one and the last one.

1036.59224.0078

ADVANCED ECONOMICS™

I like filing. Sometimes I think it's the
only thing I'm good at. In fact, even
when I'm not filing I still am; in my head.
I file everything. You should see my house.

Date:

Rel.nr:

Snce:

Ch of Com:

ADVANCED ECONOMICS™

Nr. of pages (incl. this one):   I've started to spread the rumour that my boss is having an affair with
to: his secretary. It's so much fun, all the more 'cause he is one of the
attn: most god-fearing persons around. And people are eager to believe it.

                              cons.:   from:

                    Sub: Tr.cde:
                    Re:

Trnsac.nr:
Proj: VAT nr:
                                                                Exp.
Ch of Com: Rel.nr:

                         Snce:
                         Cde: Bank acc:

ADVANCED ECONOMICS™

Employee
of the Month

1036.59224.1038

they made me
last year.
It really meant
a lot to me, but
when I came
home everybody
just laughed.

ccess, then, let me give
e simple piece of advice
d all others. Every day,
and year out, each man
ask himself, over and
ain, two questions. First,
s the name of the man I
v working for?' and
answered this definitely,
What does this man want
o, right now?'

ADVANCED ECONOMICS™

1036.59224.0046

I strongly believe a winner is a winner, and so
do most people I know in positions of influence.
There's no such thing as playing customer golf or
tennis, either with your boss or with a customer.

Every suit salesman knows he cannot sell you a
suit unless you are willing to try it on. The idea is
that once you've left your grungy old threads in the
dressing room, then fantasies of power lunches with
Donald Trump kick in, and you have sold yourself.

Experimental Jetset
Advanced Economics
1998, The Netherlands
Comprised of a collection of office supplies, Advanced Economics
is a critical examination of corporate culture, i.e., stories of
everyday misery, and is designed in a corporate style.

Audio Cassette

Lost Formats Preservation Society

Lost Formats Preservation Society

Lost Emigre57 Preservation Society

Lost Formats Preservation Society

Lost Formats Preservation Society

Lost Formats Preservation Society

Lost Formats Preservation Society

Lost Formats Preservation Society

Eight Track

Lost Formats Preservation Society

Lost Formats Preservation Society

Lost Formats Preservation Society

Lost Formats Preservation Society

Lost Formats Preservation Society

Lost Formats Preservation Society

Lost Formats Preservation Society

Lost Formats Preservation Society

Seven Inch

Lost Formats Preservation Society

Lost Formats Preservation Society

Lost Formats Preservation Society

Lost Formats Preservation Society

Lost Formats Preservation Society

Lost Formats Preservation Society

Lost Formats Preservation Society

Lost Formats Preservation Society

Video Cassette

Lost Formats Preservation Society

Lost Formats Preservation Society

Lost Formats Preservation Society

Lost Formats Preservation Society

Lost Formats Preservation Society

Lost Formats Preservation Society

Lost Formats Preservation Society

Lost Formats Preservation Society

Floppy Disc

Lost Formats Preservation Society

Lost Formats Preservation Society

Lost Formats Preservation Society

Lost Formats Preservation Society

Lost Formats Preservation Society

Lost Formats Preservation Society

Lost Formats Preservation Society

Lost Formats Preservation Society

Twelve Inch

Lost
Formats
Preservation
Society

Lost
Formats
Preservation
Society

Lost
Formats
Preservation
Society

Lost
Formats
Preservation
Society

Lost
Formats
Preservation
Society

Lost
Formats
Preservation
Society

Lost
Formats
Preservation
Society

Lost
Formats
Preservation
Society

Experimental Jetset

Six texts by respectively Jeff Khan, Andreas Angelidakis, Mihai Mamota and Ian Svenonius.

And one visual contribution by Delaware.

(About how there once was a time when every format contained its own specific data. About how nowadays the CD/DVD format is capable of containing ALL data.

And about how even this ultimate format will disappear, to make place for the final step: the mythical and platonic non-format.)

Experimental Jetset

Experimental Jetset

Six texts by respectively Jeff Khan, Andreas Angelidakis, Mihai Mamota and Ian Svenonius.

And one visual contribution by Delaware.

(About how there once was a time when every format contained its own specific data. About how nowadays the CD/DVD format is capable of containing ALL data.

And about how even this ultimate format will disappear, to make place for the final step: the mythical and platonic non-format.)

Experimental Jetset

Experimental Jetset

Six texts by respectively Jeff Khan, Andreas Angelidakis, Mihai Mamota and Ian Svenonius.

And one visual contribution by Delaware.

(About how there once was a time when every format contained its own specific data. About how nowadays the CD/DVD format is capable of containing ALL data.

And about how even this ultimate format will disappear, to make place for the final step: the mythical and platonic non-format.)

Experimental Jetset

Experimental Jetset

Experimental Jetset

Experimental Jetset

00.   01.   02.

Experimental Jetset
Lost Formats Preservation Society
Emigre #57
Winter 2000, USA
Spread for Emigre magazine in homage to lost formats, i.e., forgotten or obsolete means of storing data.

CartridgeSystem Tape ■ VinylCylinder ● Betamax ■ DigitalAudioTape ∷ DiscoVision ● MemoryStick ▮ MiniCassette ∷ Vhs Compact ■ Ditto ■ CompactVideo Cassette ■ Qic ■ SteelWireReel ⊛ Visc ● 30Channel PaperTape ○ DigitalCompactCassette ∷ Compact DiscInteractive ⊙ 18TrackTape ○ 10' VinylRecord ● DesktopHolographicDataStorage ■

MagnetoOptical Disc ■ EzFlyer ■ PaperPunchCard ■ Travan ■ Tel Dec ■ FloppyDisk ■ Phonovision ● CapacitanceElec tronicDisc ■ Neo Geo ■ VideoLong Player ● TelCan ■

8Track ■ Compac tDisc ● SuperDisk ■ 12'VinylRecord ● Viewmaster ◉ Video2000 ■ Digi talVersatileDiscR am ■ Syquest ■ U matic ■ Playtape ■ CompactFlash Card ■ DecTape ○

MiniDisc ■ Floppy Disc ◉ Magnetic AudioTape ◉ Digit alVersatileDisc ● Jaz ◆ VideoHome System ■ Video 8 ■ PocketDisc ■ DiamondDisc ● 4 Track ■ Advanced IntelligentTape ■

VideoCassetteRe cording ■ Clik! ▬ Intellivision ■ Id-1 DigitalTape ■ Sy Jet ▬ 9TrackOpen ReelTape ○ Photo Disc ● Vectrex ■ CompactCasset te ▦ SmartMedia Card ■ Telstar ▲

Experimental Jetset
Lost Formats Preservation Society
Emigre #57
Winter 2000, USA

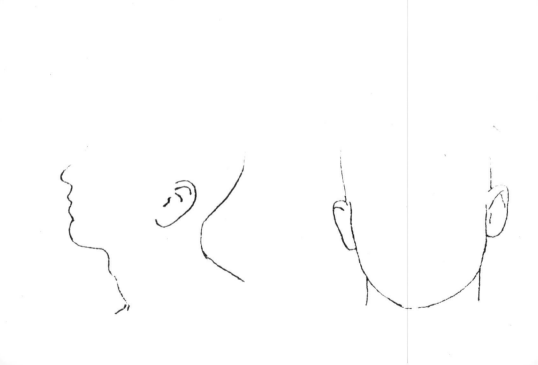

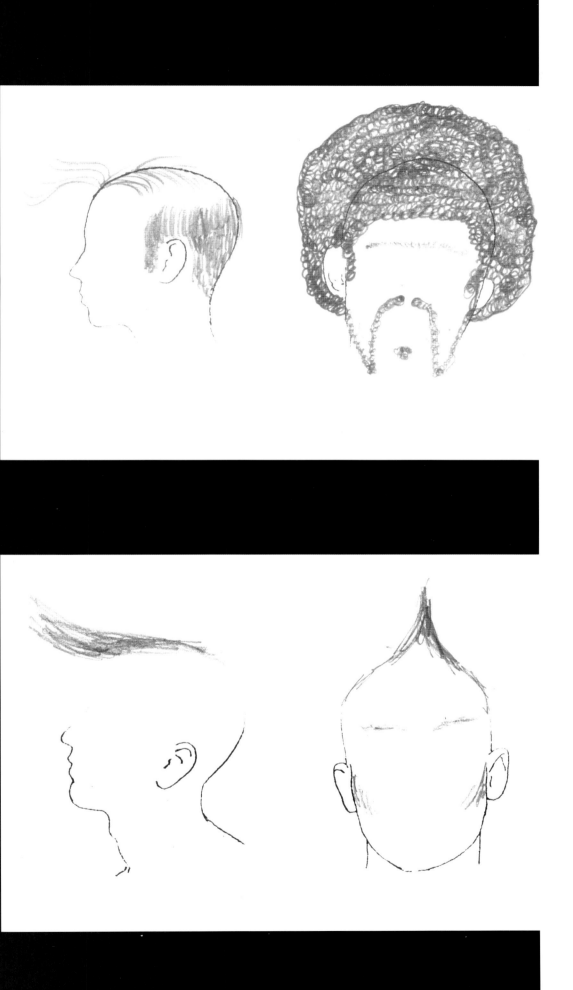

Elektrosmog PING PONG
Hairdoo card for PING PONG Raststätte;
Illustrations by Aude Lehmann
1999, Switzerland

PING PONG is a cooperative of fashion, textile and visual
designers – Andrea Roca (D.AT.UM), Franziska Born (Heimli
Feiss), Marco Walser and Valentin Hindermann (Elektrosmog).
PING PONG's first joint venture is called "Summermix", an edition
of thematic products, events and visual communication that
includes clothing (swim-suits and raincoats), embroidered
postcards and a music CD. Together, the objects are meant to
be read as a narrative of the Summer.

PING PONG is also at www.shoppingpong.ch.

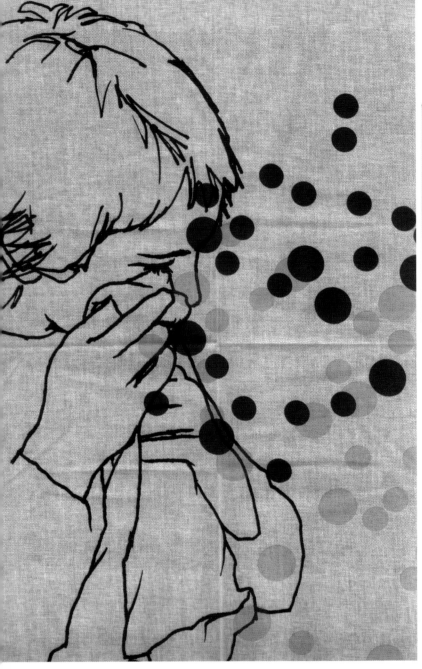

ZOR-EL & ALURA ... CONTRANA ... MELA
MINI METAL ... RJ SUMMERGRUMMER
KARLA K ... ANDY CANYON ... VASCOLOGIC
EDITH UND DER LUFTPIRAT
THE GENTS ... EIGENTON ... KAYZEE
STAUBSAUGER ... SIGNOR MUTJ
BASTIEN ... KING KAAG

PING PONG
Sommermix Edition 0.0

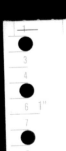

PING PONG >>> 24H RASTSTÄTTE
>>>IMBISS>>>HOT WHISKY>>>
GOTTHARDSTRASSE >>> UM DIE ECKE BEIM KONGRESSHAUS

PROGRAMM
SAMSTAG >>> PP-SCHREIBSERVICE. WIR ERLEDIGEN IHRE POST.
UND BIS 17.00>>>SOMMERFRISUREN
SAMSTAG NACHT >>> SAN KELLER GIBT WÄRME AB.
SONNTAG >>> PING PONG. DAS SPIEL. DER TREND. TOTAL.
UND>>>>>>>>>>>>>>>>>>>>>>>>>>>>>>>>>>>>>SOMMERFRISUREN

Elektrosmog
PING PONG embroidered postcards "Zimi"/"Aude"
2000, Switzerland

Elektrosmog
PING PONG handkerchief, 2000
PING PONG compilation CD "Summermix 0.0", 2000
Flyer for PING PONG
1999, Switzerland

Elektrosmog
PING PONG "Wundertüte" (surprise packet)
1999, Switzerland

Elektrosmog
PING PONG plastic bag
1999, Switzerland

Elektrosmog
Spread from PING PONG catalogue
1999, Switzerland

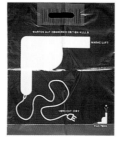

Elektrosmog
PING PONG postcard; photography by Shirana Shahbazi
2000, Switzerland

affaires culturelles

Happypets Products
"1845pts" limited-edition poster
Label Usine
February 2001, Switzerland

PUSS
GALH
(FLYI
CIRCU

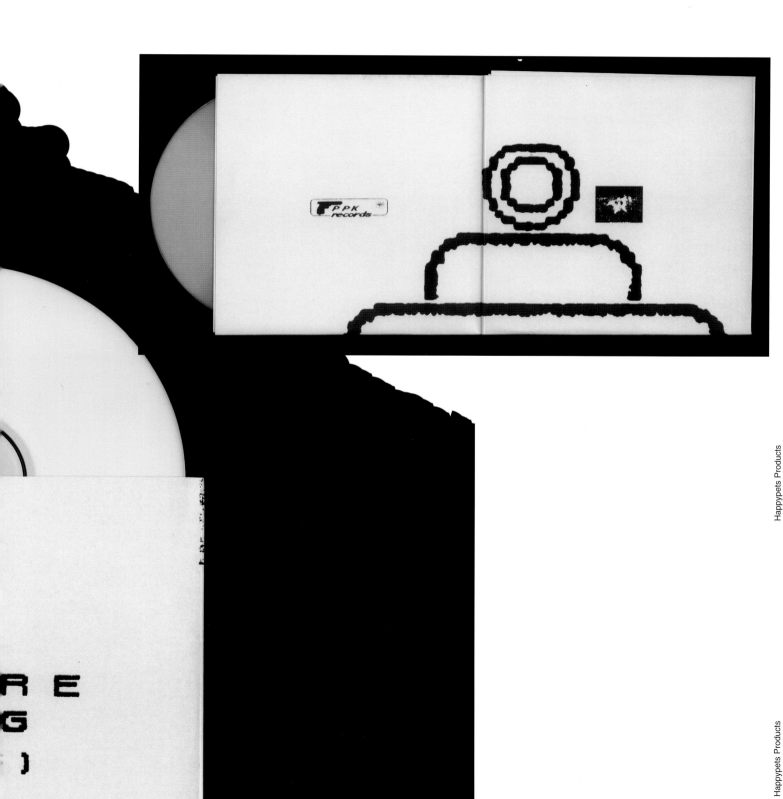

Happypets Products
CD cover and folded poster for Pussy Galhore Flying Circus
"Hawaiian tropic bikini" tour (turbolax)
Pussy Galhore
1999, Switzerland
Created with a Nintendo Gameboy printing machine.

Happypets Products
Happypets Happypeople Products identity
July 2001, Switzerland

create
desire

Happypets Products
Happypets Happypeople
July 2001, Switzerland
Animals and electronic references, such as the Macintosh's apple logo
are presented as a still-life oil painting to represent the mix of traditional
and modern graphic design tools, i.e., a fountain is shown with a path
made of mouse pads.
The smaller cards reference the Pantone colours used on dog poo bags

in Switzerland. Happypets' own white bulldog scatters hair
everywhere, and as dog hair is usually found on their artwork,
Happypets adopted it as their signature logo.

Happypets Products
Ennetna, Technological Neighbourhood
Diploma project for École Cantonale d'Art de Lausanne, by Patrick
Monnier and Violene Pont
1999/2000, Switzerland
Ennetna is a book that can be downloaded from the internet at
www.ennetna.ch, and is about people's relationships to new
communication technologies.

design refers to the intimate lives of the inhabitants. The road map format and the rather unfinished style came from the fact that the patients move from one house to another as their treatment progresses.

Happypets Products
Levant road map
Fondation du Levant
2000, Switzerland
This poster illustrates the various care houses owned by the Foundation du Levant, an association that cares for the rehabilitation of drug addicts. By focussing on the more personal details, for example pictures in bedrooms and small figurines, the

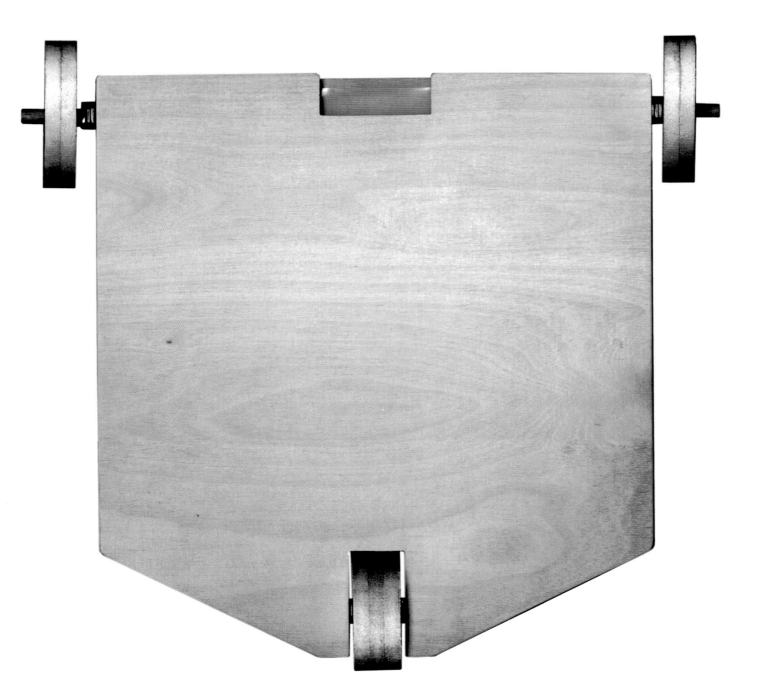

Robert Green
Seven-inch single
Headshoppe
January 2001, UK
One of 200 individually designed sleeves, by 200 different
designers. They were auctioned at the London Electricity
Showroom.

Seven easy steps to create your personalized Silas™ Summer activity poster:

1. Carefully cut around character using sharp scissors. You may wish to ask an adult to help you. 2. Open up Silas™ poster and lay flat, panoramic view facing up.
3. Use your imagination and choose where you wish to stick characters. 4. Take one character and peel off backing. 5. Carefully stick character in chosen location.
6. Repeat steps 3 through to 5 until all your characters are in position. 7. You may wish to cut speech bubbles from scraps left over and bring your characters to life.

Ben Sansbury
Silas summer activity poster and sticker sheet
Silas and Maria
March 1999, UK
Concept by Silas, illustration by James Jarvis,
design by Martin Wedderburn.

Ben Sansbury
Silas summer activity poster and sticker sheet
Silas and Maria
March 1999, UK

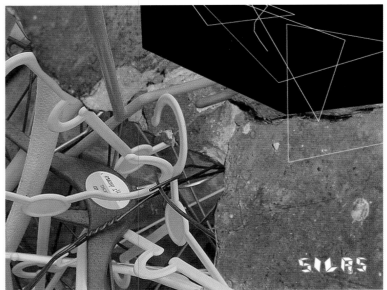

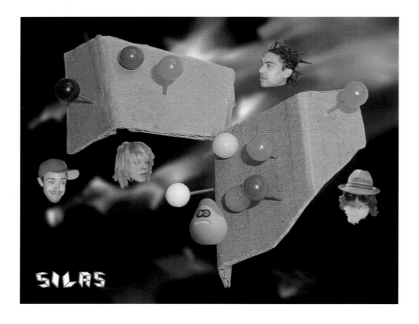

Ben Sansbury
Silas website
Silas and Maria
May 2001, UK
Art direction, design and build by Ben Sansbury and
Arron Bleasdale.

David Revell
Invitation for Mode, The Contemporary Home Show
Business Design Centre
May 1999, UK
Silver-foil blocked doiley on corrugated cardboard delivered in a
brown paper bag. Not only a preview invite this is also an elegant
thing with which to grace your dining table.

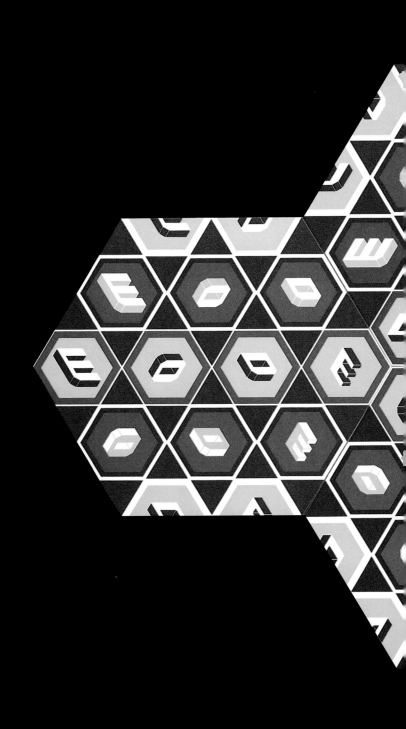

David Revell
Invitation for Mode, The Contemporary Home Show
Business Design Centre
May 1999, UK
Three-colour litho on kitschy-textured paper, to approximate
wallpaper and die-cut to echo the identity.

David Revell
Invitation for Mode, The Contemporary Home Show
Business Design Centre
May 1999, UK

SOURCE

MUSIC FESTIVAL

ALÖNE IN LONDON

ROB GEMMA HAYES KINGS OF CONVENIENCE

TURIN BRAKES

DJs FROM SOURCE

DJ AMATEUR
RECORD MAKERS, PARIS

WEDNESDAY 11 APRIL 2001

7PM UNTIL 1AM
TICKETS: £8

, KINGSLAND VIADUCT
83 RIVINGTON St
SHOREDITCH, LONDON, EC2

TUBES: OLD STREET
LIVERPOOL STREET

ON THE DOOR OR
IN ADVANCE FROM

XFM TICKET LINE TEL 0870 160 1000
WWW.TICKETWEB.CO.UK, TEL 020 7771 2000

www.crasta-london.com

WWW.SOURCELAB.NET
WWW.ALONEINLONDON.NET
INFO@ALONEINLONDON.NET

XfM
104.9
LONDON

JOCKEY SLUT
MAGAZINE

i-gig.com
live and online

SLEAZENATION
MAGAZINE

SOURCE 360

"WORDPLAY"

äbäke
"Alone in London" poster for the Source Festival
Source UK
April 2001, UK

The design is a response to the French head of Source UK,
Philippe Ascoli's love of the Britain way of life. With his complaints
about the weather, food and traffic, äbäke felt he was in spirit a true
anglophile and in many ways more British than the British. So, they
created a non-traditional British crest of his own.

Perrier-Jouët Selfridges
Design Prize

ābäke
Poster for the Perrier-Jouët Selfridges Design Prize
Perrier-Jouët/Selfridges
2000, UK

âbäke
CD sampler
Source France
May 2001, France

Based on the ideas behind their design for the British label, âbäke's design for Source France uses ubiquitous vintage fonts, such as Banco and Choc designed by Roger Excoffon and commonly seen in French signage during the 1950s and 1960s.

âbäke
CD sampler
Source UK
March 2001, UK

äbäke
Welcoming wallpaper
2000, UK
Designed for an exhibition organised for the London launch of the
US underwear company Joe Boxer.

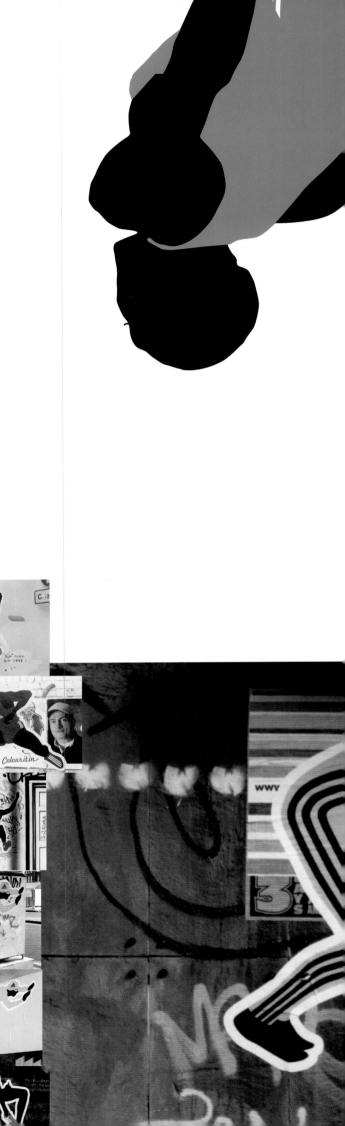

Big Corporate Disco
Street Olympics
Adidas
September 2000, UK
Life-sized die-cut flyposters highlighting Adidas's sponsorship of the
British Olympic team. Instructions were given to paste the action
shots at appropriate heights, i.e., the high-jumper always appears
over six feet off the ground and the hurdler at three feet.

MAJOR INCIDENT

OCCURRING ON APRIL 22ND
**BETWEEN 9AM - 5PM
INVOLVING 35,000 PEOPLE**

RUNNING **26.2** MILES FROM BLACKHEATH
IN THE DIRECTION OF SW1

Big Corporate Disco
Marathon road signs
Adidas
April 2001, UK
Dummy warning signs screen-printed onto correx were placed
along the route of the London Marathon to highlight Adidas's
involvement as an official sponsor.

Big Corporate Disco
Euro 2000
Adidas
2001, UK
Silk-screened scoreboards for the Euro 2000 semi-final matches
were reproduced on walls around London, inviting fans to guess
the scores of upcoming fixtures.

The Chocolate Factory.
Open Studios 2000

100+ artists, across a variety of artforms at The Chocolate Factory, North London's most vibrant arts experience.

Saturday 25 November
Sunday 26 November
12.00pm – 6.00pm

Entrance £1 (children free)

Haringey Arts Council
The Chocolate Factory
Clarendon Road, Wood Green
London N22 6XJ

T 020 8365 7500
F 020 8365 8686
E hac@teleregion.co.uk

⊖ Wood Green
BR Alexandra Palace
Bus W3

HARINGEY ARTS COUNCIL
HARINGEY COUNCIL

Design automatic

Automatic
Young at Art Awards 2001 poster pack and invitation
The London Institute/Young at Art
2000, UK

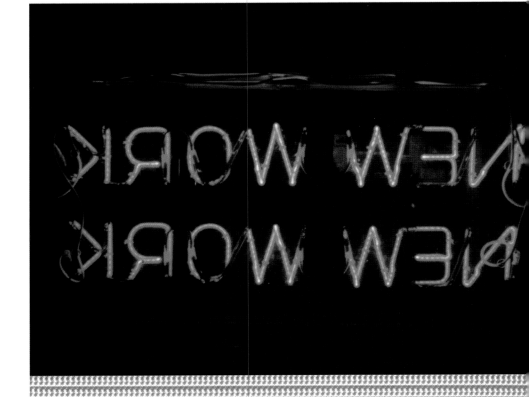

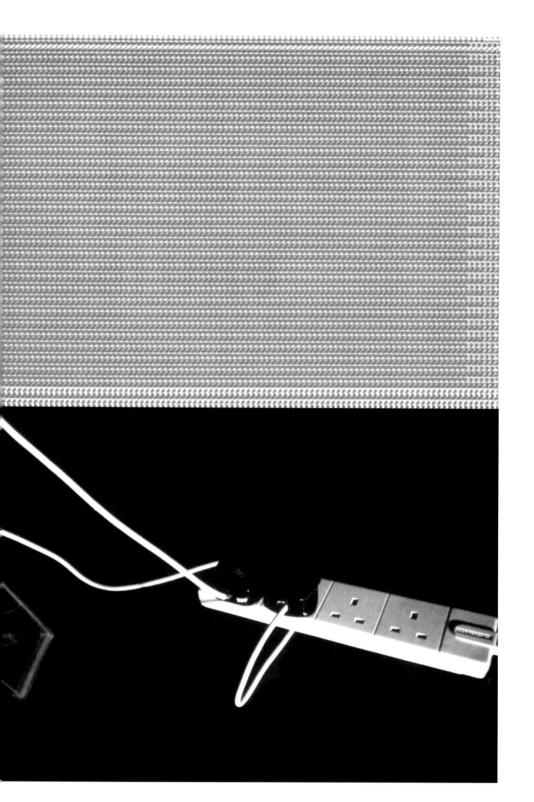

Automatic and Richard Bonner-Morgan
"New Work New Work" catalogue for Degree Show
Kingston University
2000, UK

gareth tansey
digital designer

tel 079 777 48386

SARAH POWELL

The Bitch Works Hard

21 Farmington Road,
Cheltenham, GL51 6AG
Tel: 0780 3844451

"it's communication baby!"

pauline lock
Tel: 07977 117287

SAM WILSON
IMAGE CREATER

GRAPHIC ILLUSTRATOR
June Cottage, 251 Main Road, Walters Ash
01494 564849

Located at:High Wycombe HP14 4TH
SEE ME FOR THE IMAGE YOU DESIRE

ENGERLAND

Susan and Catherine

One degree under but not for long!

c/o Buckinghamshire Chilterns University College
High Wycombe
Tel: 01494 522141

PAULA AND VICKY

WISH WE WERE HERE!

BUCKINGHAMSHIRE UNIVERSITY COLLEGE
QUEEN ALEXANDRA ROAD, HIGH WYCOMBE
Tel: 01494 522141

Advertising is our second favourite thing.

Kristian & Mark

07957 474733

I CAN COOK AS WELL!

I can also Salsa dance, wash up, and garden

Charlie Jobson

Tel: EVERYONE!!
07801 721610

BISH

GRAPHIC ILLUSTRATOR
MARK BISHOP

Uni 01494 459886

Tel: 01323 422205

---

h-r-r-oann
ur-r-ol-Nin
oa N)|N(
(zyx-wvuts-ruwqrt

Start spreading the neeews,
We're leaving todaaay...

Sarah & Alison
Advertising Creatives
Tel: 07957 193869 / 07801 709998

Easy

Gary lathwell (art director)
Call: 01525 713205

0

7957 461494

---

 a diamond amongst the rough

lesley waters
Tel: 07957227217

 HUMA MUSHTAQ

a bright spark

---

damo

JACK OF ALL TRADES, MASTER OF NONE

T 01543 432287
P 04325 235956

The average student team
spend 18mths on the street looking for a job

FCUK THAT!

Jo & Caf
BA(Hons) ADVERTISING

INSERT MONEY

IAN WALLER
0403 968 908

CARRIE-LOUISE WEBB
TEL: 0797 9470745

Meet me before you.
meet anyone else,
so you don't feel sorry
that you met me last.

SKYDIVING INSTRUCTORS

GUY & AL
Lying bastards
Tel: 0403 510 627

Rob & Ad*

creatives

07957 123519
* subject to availability

 JULES & SI

HUNT US DOWN

tel:07801 351 256
email:n6990108@buckscol.ac.uk
these are the creatives you're looking for

NEW HORIZONS

graphic designer

Michelle Richardson
Tel: 07957 243842
TAKING DESIGN TO NEW HORIZONS

RMH DESIGNS

Rose M Hall
Nee Gibson

2 Norfolk Court
28 Norfolk Road
Maidenhead, Berks

Tel: 01628 628253
Fax: 01628 628253
RoseMHall@Compuserve

R JUDD
...esigner/Illustrator

...there's more to the
...an just porn..."

...cer@hotmail.com
...6433

THE EAGLE HAS LANDED
GRAPHIC DESIGNER

YEWHUNG CHIN
Tel: 01494 461 043
0956 341 803
DON'T FALL PREY TO OTHERS!

Undiscovered, attractive female, GSOH,

looking for perfect partner to share good times etc...

Tel: Call Clare on O956 53O69O

TODAY'S SPECIAL

JESSICA CHANEY
01703 230 546

PLAYER
...rphy

SOLUTIONS

...4 782881

...e Colour. Blue
...e Day. Wednesday
...e Drink. Ribena
...e Food. Pizza

NO JOB TOO BIG!
call EMMA SIMONS NOW

on 07957 223210

FOR ALL YOUR GRAPHIC DESIGN NEEDS

Chris Watling
design underdog

Tel: 01268 663152

Tel: 0402528972

GEEZERS

We 'ave 59 business cards for sale
Your name doesn't have to be MEL or ADAM
(but it would help)

V.G.C. But real bad quali'y
and at 2wenny p each, it's a steal
Call me man on 07899 694626
Sweet

SHELLY

...ads in horse riding, manioures &
...fumes.
...7 193860

...I to book a time when we're not
...ing.

Carole Walters

8 Townsend Road, Needingworth
Huntingdon, Cambridgeshire
Fax:01480 497634
Tel:01480 466165

Fiona Strange

"What's in a name?" Shakespeare

Tel: 01582 650773
Mobile: 0958 343355

PAUL THURLBY
Graphic Illustrator & Caricaturist Extraordinaire

NO BIG HEADS AND SMALL BODIES
(I LIKE MY WOMEN IN PROPORTION!)

Tel: 0115 9821798

Sañsôme
Filmaker

...gger

...SHED
...FIELD
...ERZET
...49 870684

LUCKY CATCH
Graphic Designer

Raymond Luck

Tel: 01992 589891
Mob: 07803 265276

ELLA WILSON - COPY   WRITER

CAROLINE OLIVER
ART DIREKTOR   01494 513321

...th Jones
...Designer Royale

...ie

...Cottage
...ethe
...ester
...69 277689

Sir Giles Winser
Advertising Guru

South London
01372 464527
Full of ideas ready to blow

CATHERINE SULLIVAN

0631 751284

---

matt strong
Digital film maker

Strong ideas

92 VALENTINES WAY ROMFORD ESSEX

WILLING TO LEARN
Tel: 0181 593 0451

JIM SMITH
I'll TAKE YOUR PHOTO BABY!

TEL: 01935863702

OR SALE
...d Speed Racer

...l gift, v.good condition, royal blue,
...d lights inc. £50 o.n.o
...p on 0378 124 831

---

stuart hobbs
Graphic designer

Graphic troubleshooter

(01749) 678633
OR (01494) 439141

THE SKY'S THE LIMIT
Gareth Twine

Conceptual Illustrator
Tel:07971915686

Woof! Woof!
3 year old puppies for sale

Very well trained, lively, faithful to owners.
Dog answers to the name Rowan,
Claire answers to the name of bitch.

You'll be barking mad to miss them.
TEL. 07957 348219

Nigel Robinson
Poster and private view invitation for the Graphic Design,
Illustration and Advertising Degree Show
Buckinghamshire Chilterns University College
1999, UK

Rob & Ad*

creatives

07957 123519

*subject to availability

JULES & SI

HUNT US DOWN

tel:07801 351 256
email:n6990108@buckscol.ac.uk
these are the creatives you're looking for

Michelle Richardson
Tel: 07957 243842
TAKING DESIGN TO NEW HORIZONS

Rose M Hall

Nee Gibson

2 Norfolk Court   Tel: 01628 628253
28 Norfolk Road   Fax: 01628 628253
Maidenhead, Berks   RoseMHall@Compuserve

Susan and Catherine

One degree under but not for long!

c/o Buckinghamshire Chilterns University College
High Wycombe
Tel: 01494 522141

DAVE GUMBLE

It takes true BCUC style and wit
To create a poster design this shit.
My student friends, I will truly miss,
As for this college - are you taking the piss?

---

damo

JACK OF ALL TRADES, MASTER OF NONE

T 01543 432287
P 04325 235956

IDEAS FOR SALE*

-Available in all sizes (small shown here)
-All brand new

For a brochure call:
James Anderson-Hanney
(01705) 297238   *subject to availability

FOR SALE

...h 16 Speed Racer

Graphic designer

Graphic troubleshooter

(01749) 678633
OR (01494) 439141

THE SKY'S THE LIMIT

Gareth Twine

Conceptual Illustrator
Tel:07971915686

Woof! Woof!

3 year old puppies for sale

Very well trained, lively, faithful to owners.
Dog answers to the name Rowan,
Claire answers to the name of bitch.

You'll be barking mad to miss them.
TEL. 07957 348219

...our second favourite thing.

Kristian & Mark

07957 474733

Private View Invitation
Buckinghamshire Chilterns University

Degree Show 1999

Department of Graphic Design
Illustration & Advertising
FRIDAY 25TH JUNE 1999
From 5.30PM-8.00PM

Buckinghamshire Chilterns University College
Queen Alexandra Road, High Wycombe,
Buckinghamshire HP11 2JZ

Graphic Design, Illustration & Advertising
Degree Show 1999

Private View: Friday 25th June 5.30 pm - 8.00 pm
Sunday 27th June 10.00 am - 2.00 pm
Monday 28th June - Wednesday 30th June 10.00 am - 8.00 pm
Thursday 1st July 10.00 am - 4.00 pm

Nigel Robinson
Poster and private view invitation for the Graphic Design,
Illustration and Advertising Degree Show
Buckinghamshire Chilterns University College
1999, UK

ROYAL COLLEGE OF ART
SCHOOL OF COMMUNICATIONS
COMMUNICATION ART AND DESIGN
SUMMER SHOW 00

OPENING TIMES
THURSDAY 29 JUNE - MONDAY 10 JULY
10AM - 6PM DAILY
(CLOSED JULY 7)

PRIVATE VIEW
WEDNESDAY 28 JUNE

LOWER GALLERIES
ROYAL COLLEGE OF ART
KENSINGTON GORE
LONDON SW7 2EU

TELEPHONE +44 (0)20 7590 4498
FAX +44 (0)20 7590 4300
E-MAIL info@rca.ac.uk
www.rca.ac.uk

THIS IS NOT A PRIVATE VIEW TICKET

Royal College of Art
Postgraduate Art & Design

Jon Hares and Sean Murphy
Invitation to Degree Show
Royal College of Art
2000, UK

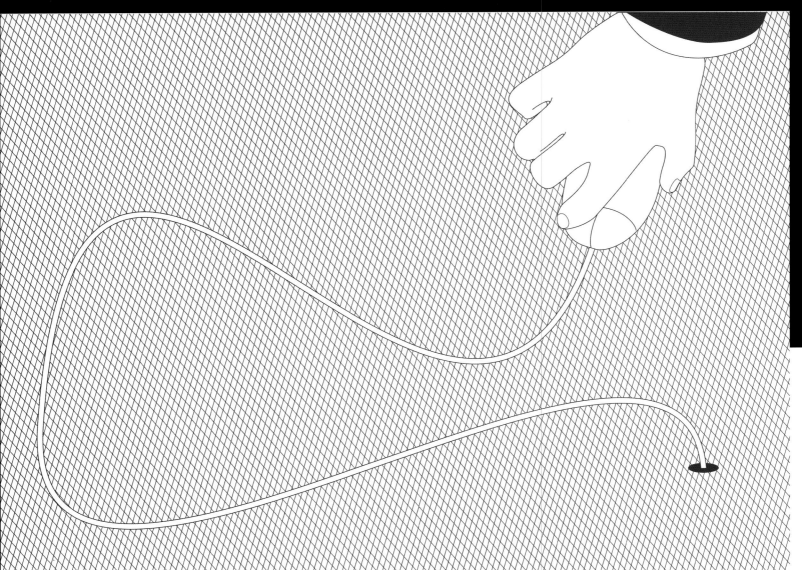

ELEVEN

WORK

AN EXHIBITION OF ELEVEN NEW ARCHITECTS AND DESIGNERS

PRIVATE VIEW   1st FEBRUARY 2001
EXHIBITION   2nd - 9th FEBRUARY 2001

138 KINGSLAND ROAD E2

ALIAS _ GAMPERMARTINO
CLEO BRODA
CRISPIN JONES
DLM
EMULSION
FLATLIFE
HARES
HELEN EVANS / HEIKO HANSEN
SCOTTBOYENS
SEXYMACHINERY
TCA

Sponsored by

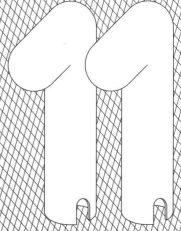

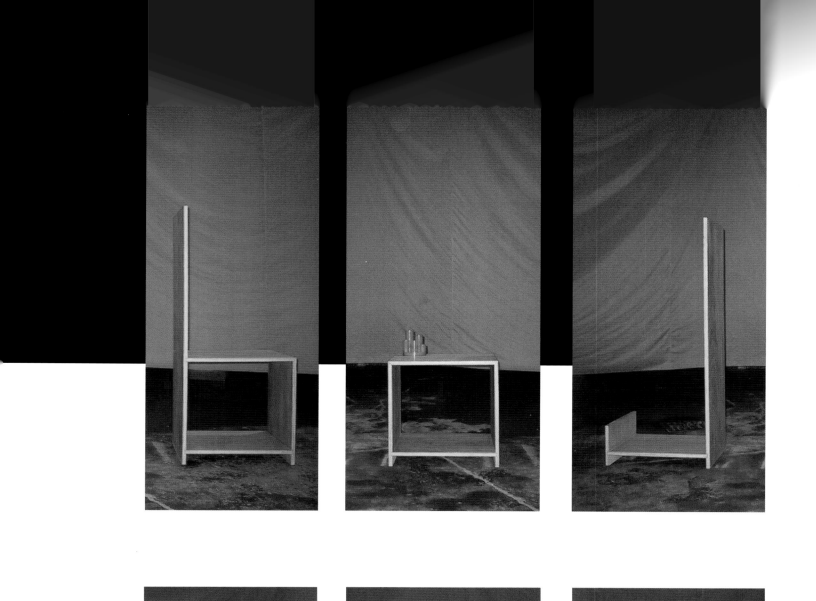

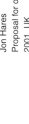

Jon Hares
Proposal for office furniture, (Job)
2001, UK

and fold-out catalogue

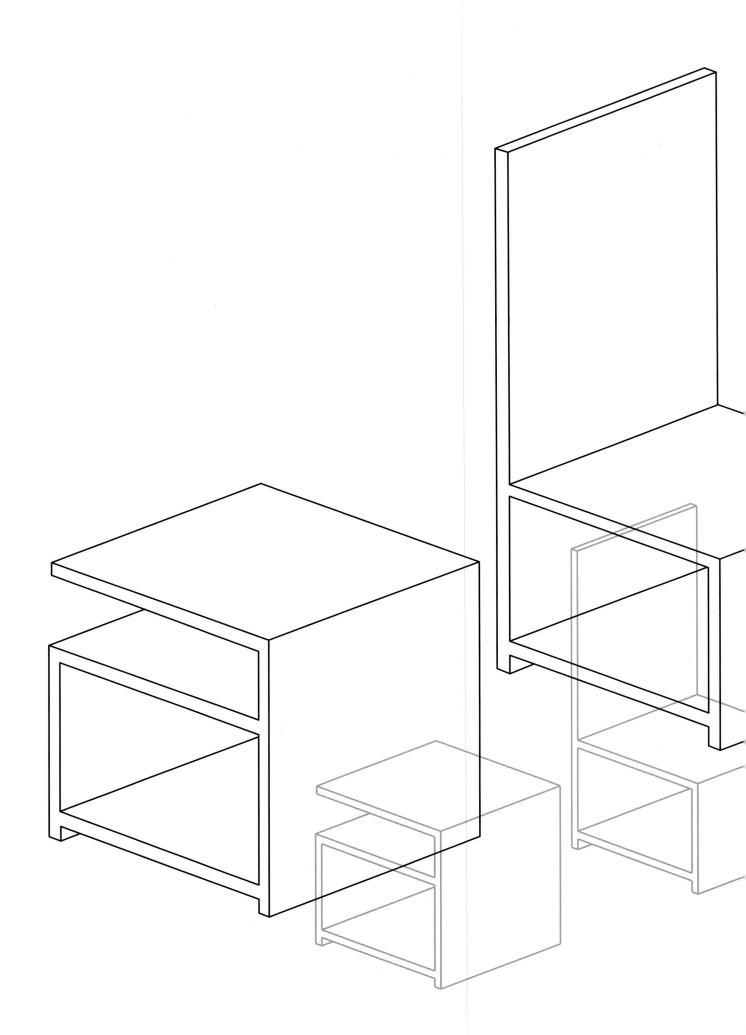

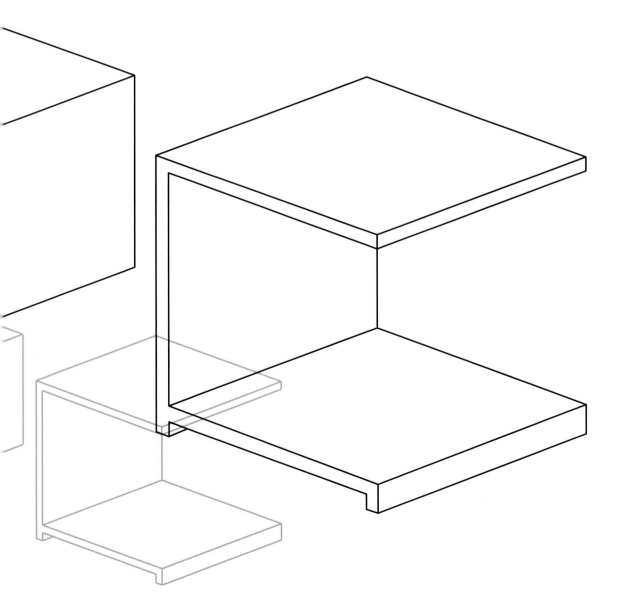

Jon Hares
Proposal for office furniture, (Job)
2001, UK

Published by
Royal College of Art
Kensington Gore
London SW7 2EU

Design Products Department
T +44 020 7590 4322
F +44 020 7590 4280
E design@rca.ac.uk
www.designproducts.rca.ac.uk

Photograph by
Ruth Farrington

Portrait by
Dara Arad

Drawings by
Rei Terao

Printed by
New Image, London

ISBN 1 874175 63 2

Thank you
Maki Suzuki, Kajsa Ståhl, Nigel Shafran, Mini Rich, Michael Marriott,
James Goggin, Hilary French, Durrel Bishop and Laurent Benner

Maki Suzuki and Kajsa Ståhl, London 2000

Alex Rich
Thank you 1
2001, UK
Page in the Annual of the Design Products Department at the Royal
College of Art, designed by Alex Rich. After loosing the entire book
from his computer the day before it was due to go to print, Rich
called on friends Maki Suzuki and Kajsa Ståhl to help him redesign
the book. The page is a tribute to their help and friendship.

Alex Rich, James Goggin, Philippe Desarzens and Laurent Benner
Thank you 2
2000, Switzerland

I ♥ Peanut Butter, Switzerland

Lunch, Austria

Please, Austria

Fake Moustache, Switzerland

Two Landscapes, Switzerland

Fence, London

Airplane, London

Souvenir of Finsbury Park, London

Greetings, Switzerland

Almost / Nearly works 1997 –

Alex Rich
Almost/nearly work
1997-2001, various locations

Ohio Girl, Andy Mueller
"Exit Now" sleeve design for National Skyline
File 13 Records
2000, USA

NATIONAL SKYLINE

NATIONAL SKYLINE
THIS=EVERYTHING ...

Ohio Girl, Andy Mueller
Poster for CD cover
File 13 Records
2000, USA

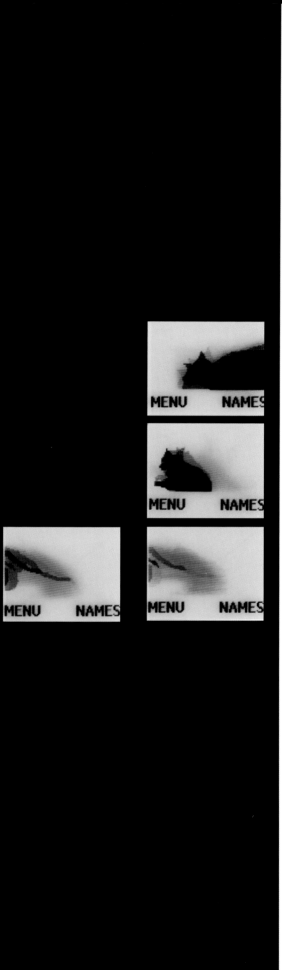

Graphic Thought Facility

Detail of lenticulars for Project #26765 – FLIRT: flexible information

and recreation for mobile users

Royal College of Art/Computer Related Design

2000, UK

The lenticulars were used to illustrate an animation on the screen

of a mobile phone.

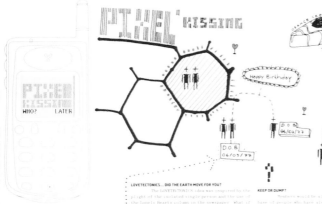

PIXEL KISSING

WHO? LATER

● ESPRESSO TO GO
Attract: press M31, wants to
stay up late & chat, sometimes
coffee & grappa, with witty,
intellig attract F 25-35.

PH+SR

EXIT OK EXIT REMIND M...

CELLULAR NEARNESS

PIXEL KISSING is a social experiment exploring virtual communities in real space. It uses locational proximity and data coincidence to create *cellular nearness* between members. When members of the same virtual community are present in the same cell, both receive a PIXEL KISSING signal, alerting them to the other's presence. They will not have met physically so will not be able to identify who that person is, only that they are somewhere close by.

1 DAY IN 365

At an early concept stage we had been playing with ideas of strangers and coincidence. If it happened to be your birthday, throughout the day anyone who happened to have a birthday on the same day would greet you via your phone. Of course they would remain anonymous and most likely would not be in the immediate vicinity - perhaps they would be walking on the street around the corner - but in the recipient's mind the caller could be anyone around them. A little more information, like birth year and gender, would fuel the imagination even more.

LOVETECTONICS... DID THE EARTH MOVE FOR YOU?

The LOVETECTONICS idea was inspired by the plight of the isolated single person and the use of the lonely hearts column in the newspaper. What if this service became locational and the description of a potential partner's location could be sent...

SERIOUS TOOL OF LOVE OR A MULTI-USER GAME?

As we developed these ideas for the focus group, we began to wonder if our lonely hearts service was a serious tool for love or simply a fun game based on multi-users...

KEEP OR DUMP?

Members would be allowed access to a database of people who have also left adverts in that location, and would be able to choose up to a maximum of five potential partners...

CELLULAR HEARTBEATS

Using the PIXEL KISSING concept, heart beats would be sent out when a member shared a cell with one of their chosen five...

PROTAGONIST IN THE 'HERE AND NOW'

As several locative patterns begin to emerge in a certain place at a regular time, ideas about particular times and locations become significant...

IT'S ALL IN THE IMAGINATION

It was important to us that the people could actually get to meet, like a detective story...

NO-MAN'S LAND OF MOBILITY

As our ideas progressed, we began to realise that the potential existed for this technology to become something more vital...

ANONYMOUS COLLECTIVES

To what extent could the presence of certain strangers in the LOVETECTONICS game reach a level of closeness comparable to a network of close friends, but still remain anonymous?...

THE PIXEL KISSING SOCIETY

The next trial in Helsinki to test out all the components of the technical system is an opportunity to find out what might happen with a group of strangers in a city of a million, where...

GRADUAL ENCOUNTERS. IT TAKES TI...

We attempted to structure the progression of the virtual friendships so that first, second and third meetings became more intimate...

TIGHT MESH? ERRANT TANGLE?

The main focus of the LOST CAT is that people would be aware of the...

ACKNOWLEDGEMENTS

I would like to thank all our partners in this project, particularly the pivotal Dave Bell, project manager from Philips Research Labs, and the software team: Dave Yule, Nigel Byrnes, Dave Walker, Paul Simons. From Infogrames: Christophe Comparin, Richard Bottet, Aurélien Telmon. From Helsinki Telephone Corporation: Timo Flinkkila, Juha Sundell. All the members of the RCA design team particularly Ben Hooker, who has played a central role, Neil Clavin, Nick Durrant, Paul Farrington, Marcus Gosling, Shona Kitchen, Arita Patel, Niall Sweeny, Brendan Walker. In addition we thank Akira Suzuki, Claire Catterall, Giles Lane, Gillian Crampton Smith, Andrew Stevens from GTF, and for endless inspiration, Anthony Dunne.

Fiona Raby (Project Leader)

Design: Graphic Thought Facility
Print: Ventura Litho Ltd
Lenticular production: Jake Purches

Object photography: Angela Moore
Helsinki photography: Timo Flinkkila
Crowd photography: Lubna Hammoud

MENU   NAMES

PARALLEL WORLDS CROSS OVER

As well as investigations into sociality we are doing a number of experiments we are calling 'the epic and the everyday'. These deal with overlaying surreal fictional narratives between the city and the parallel virtual data landscape, attempting to blur the two worlds, and create a dynamic where they stimulate each other.

EVENT-BASED SIGNALLING

In the early conceptual stage, we were interested in how random events could be generated by the activities of the city, such as the arrival of the Trans-Siberian train into Helsinki every Thursday morning, key temperatures, when the sea begins to freeze, the start of the ice hockey season. We imagined how these different city events could be linked to objects and spaces within virtual space, so that when the city changes the virtual space changes - a large plane arriving at Helsinki airport causes a thunderstorm to occur, when the sea freezes, certain virtual pathways in a game become blocked while others open up. But at this stage our idea was all very vague and undefined and not quite making sense.

SHIFTING SCALES

We overlaid a map of Los Angeles over Helsinki to compare the cities. We enjoyed the juxtaposition of the two scales and the coincidences between which districts happened to lie on top of each other, and imagined that different game spaces might have different space-time properties. On some days a walk across the city would be the equivalent to walking a few metres in game space, while on other days it might represent millions of miles over thousands of years.

This idea of two spaces existing together simultaneously in parallel universes intrigued us. And the idea that every now and again the two worlds would cross over was something we wanted to investigate more.

AN AUTONOMOUS BEING

The LOST CAT, one of our trial experiments, played with this idea. A virtual creature, living and roaming around Helsinki's cellular telephone network, occasionally jumps onto people's mobile screens. Originally we imagined that if you feed the cat and return to the same place at the same time, the cat will befriend you. Over time it will grow fatter and happier, purring louder and becoming more friendly. Eventually, if you continue to feed it, it starts to follow you and appear on your phone when you least expect it. Like real cats it will wander and lie all over other information on your display. And like real cats, which are independent creatures, if you neglect it, it will wander off and find someone else to love it.

FAKING IT

We couldn't have a real cat so we had to fake one across the network, imagining movement through the network...

IT GETS BORED

We wanted the cat to no longer be a passive creature, so in the second version there is a call for it to be fed. If they have not fed it, the phone rings for a short time and if you answer it will no longer be there...

REV...

MENU

LOST CAT

◀ FIELD STUDY #2 — LOST CAT & STAMPEDE

PRAVO

SOAP

WE ARE CURIOUS...

CAT CRUELTY

MENU   NAMES

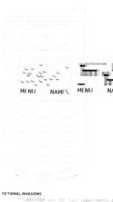

MENU   NAMES

MENU   NAMES

MENU   NAMES

FICTIONAL INVASIONS

WE ARE CURIOUS...

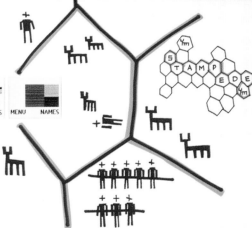

STAMPEDE

NEXT TIME...

WE ARE CURIOUS...

Graphic Thought Facility
Project #26765 — FLIRT: flexible information and recreation for mobile users
Royal College of Art/Computer Related Design
2000, UK

MUF

'Pleasure Garden of the Utilities', 1999. Ceramic bench test pieces.

'Pleasure Garden of the Utilities' is a project for Stoke City Council to resuscitate an unwelcoming street corner in Hanley, Stoke-on-Trent. muf collaborated with local manufacturers Armitage Shanks to create a ceramic bench decorated with chinoiserie-style blue flowers. The idea was to celebrate the communal nature of the site by creating something that 'belonged' to the area and the people. The scheme draws on Stoke's industrial heritage, using traditional motifs and local skills.

muf is a collaborative practice of architects and artists who effectively push against the boundaries of received architectural practice. The main tenet of their work is to implement strategies which recognise that architecture must extend beyond its built limit. Committed to working in the public realm, they aim to establish enduring and meaningful interventions on the social and cultural as well as the physical fabric of the urban environment. A keyword is inclusivity—all projects involve consultation, negotiation and collaboration with local communities. Beginning with a thorough examination of the community's needs, hopes and dreams, muf actively seek out those things that usually remain hidden, marginalised or censored out as a means to facilitate a true sense of ownership.

Name: **MUF**

Please keep your answers to a maximum of 15 words.

Who do you design for? (Ideally).
YOU / HE / THEM & RAESY MOON

What effect do you like your work to have?
CALMLY / SOMETHING IN BETWEEN VIOLENT
MOVING / SLAUGHTER & GENTLE MELANCHOLY

Who/what has inspired you?
FRESH AIR / BEING IN LOVE & ANIMALS

Who/what inspires you now?
POLY STYREEN / ANIMALS

What is your favourite material and/or process at the moment?
STONE / DIALOGUE / LOOKING / RENAMING

Who/what would be your ideal client/commission be?
A RAILWAY STATION, AN ICE RINK FOR A PENINSULA IN
THE NORTHERN HEMISPHERE, & A HOUSING PROJECT FOR 6000 PEOPLE

What do you avoid in design?
'DESIGN' / DOING CRAP WORK

What is your first design memory?
MILTON KEYNES / MY FATHER'S DIY

What is your worst design memory?
CAN'T REMEMBER / THE CONCEPT OF DESIGN MEMORY

What's the worst word anybody could use (or has used) to describe your work?
THOUGHTLESS

Where have you found beauty in the ordinary and everyday?
HERE, THERE AND EVERYWHERE

What was the last thing you stole?
SUGAR / A GLANCE

Describe/draw a favourite object.

Robbie Mahoney
Paper sizes poster
2000, UK

SIAN RUSSELL
TEXTILES EMBROIDERY PRINT

ABC

Robbie Mahoney
Promotional poster for embroiderer Sian Russell
2001, UK

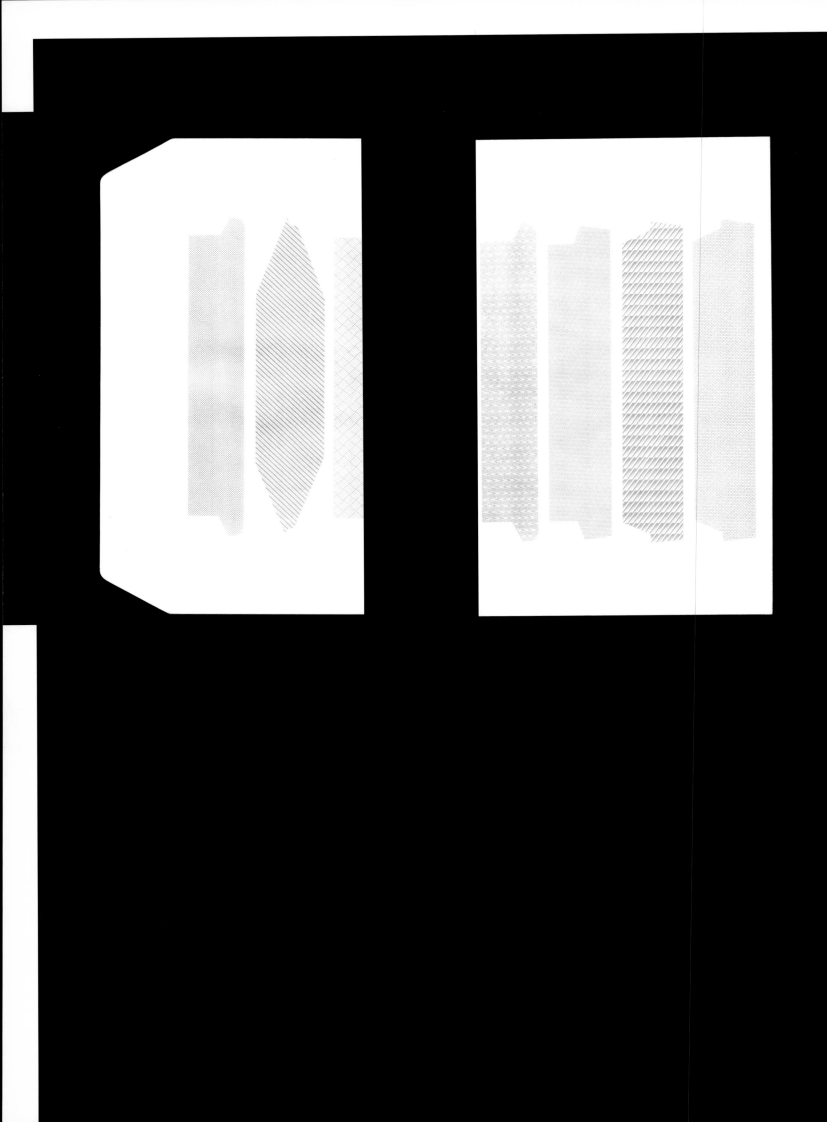

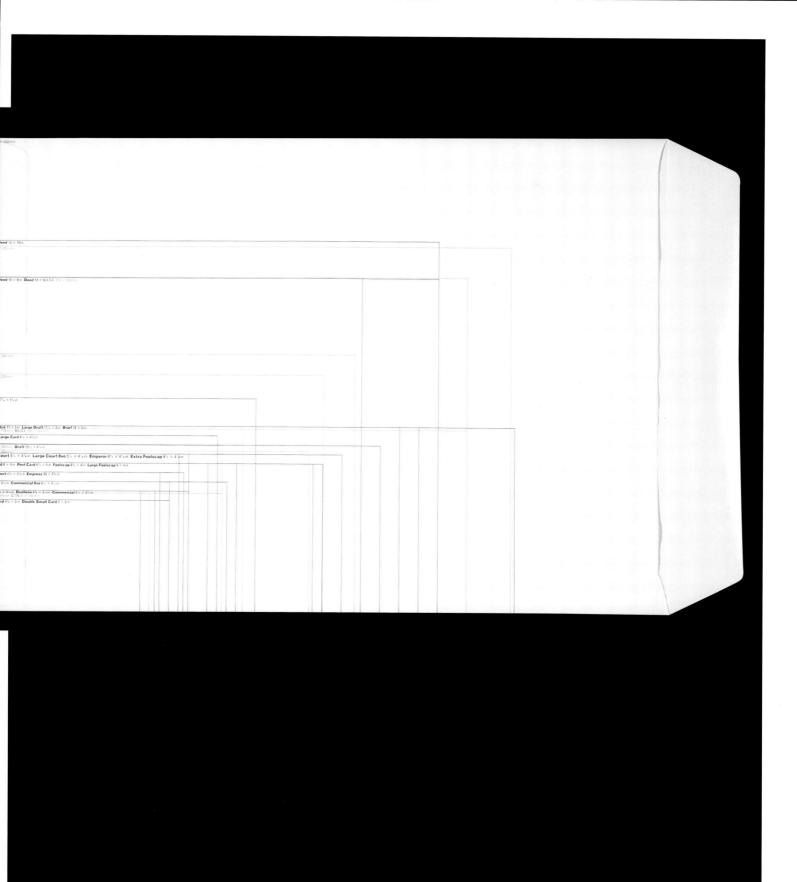

Robbie Mahoney
Envelope sizes envelopes
2001, UK

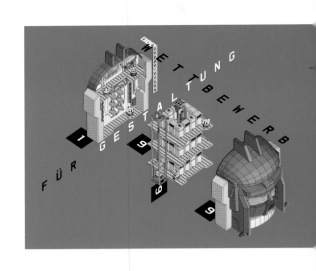

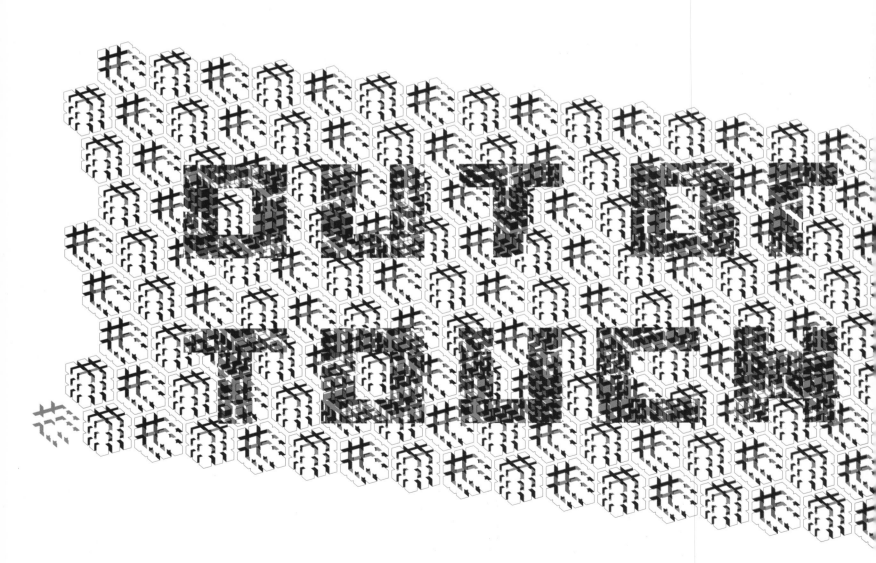

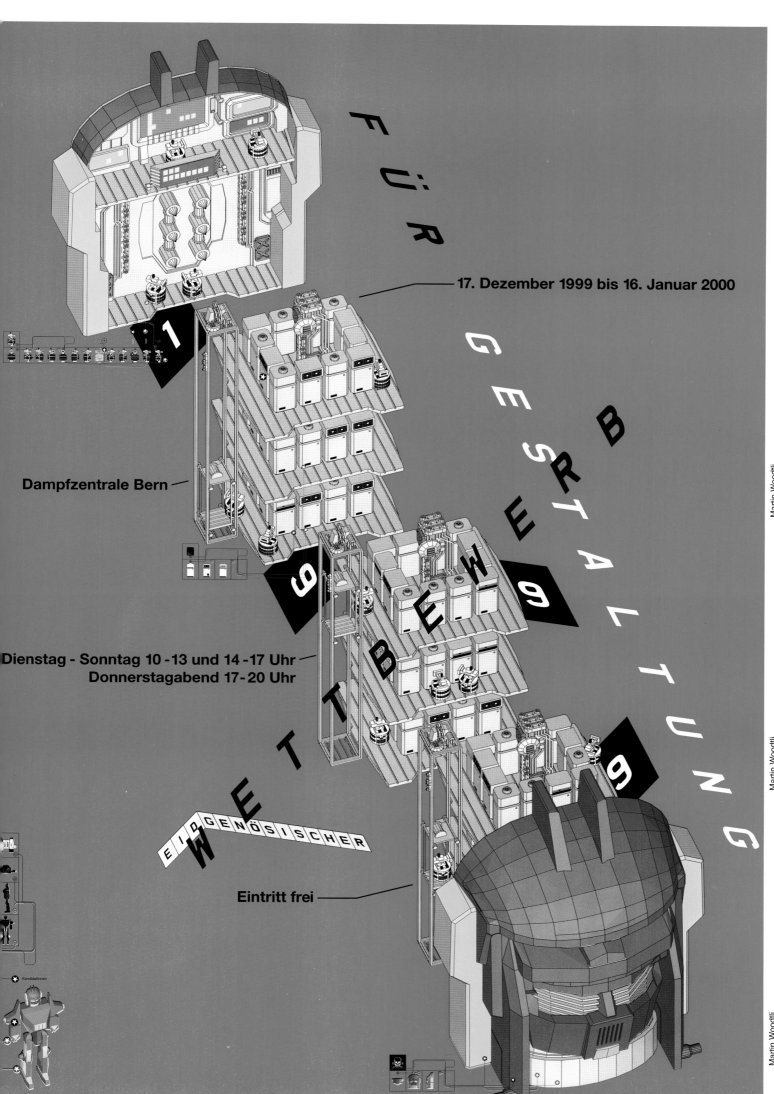

F Ü R

G E S T A L

17. Dezember 1999 bis 16. Januar 2000

Dampfzentrale Bern

Dienstag - Sonntag 10 -13 und 14 -17 Uhr
Donnerstagabend 17- 20 Uhr

EIDGENÖSISCHER

Eintritt frei

W E T T B E W E

T U N G

Martin Woodtli
Flyer for Eidgenössicher Wettbewerb für Gestaltung und Kunst
Bundesamt für Kultur
November 1999, Switzerland

Martin Woodtli
Poster for Eidgenössicher Wettbewerb für Gestaltung und Kunst
Bundesamt für Kultur
November 1999, Switzerland

Martin Woodtli
"Out of Touch" flyers for an art gallery
Stadtgalerie Bern
January 2001, Switzerland

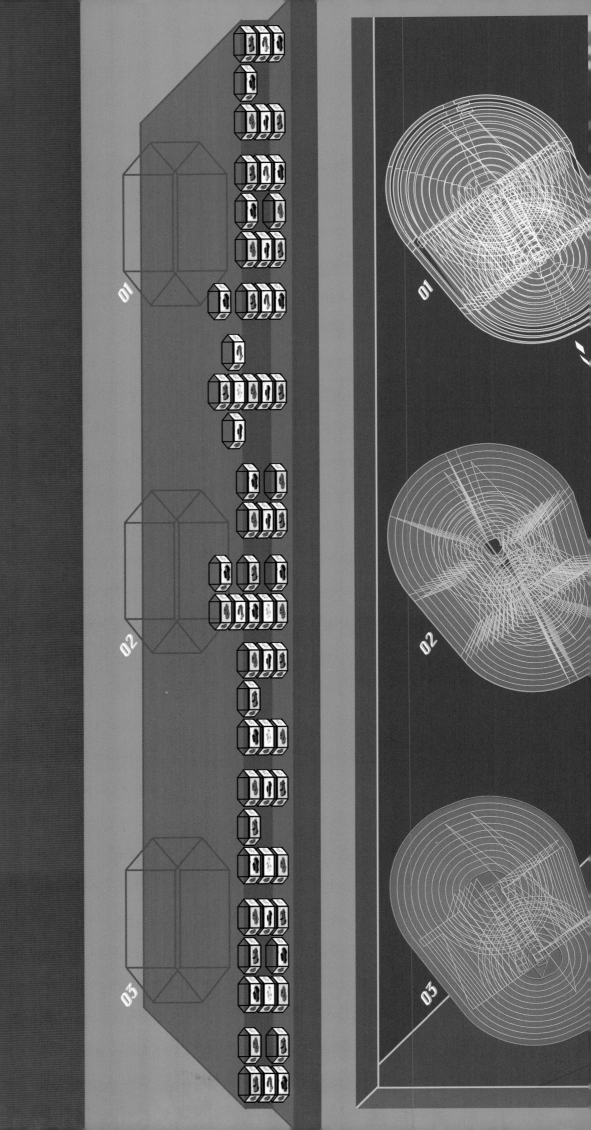

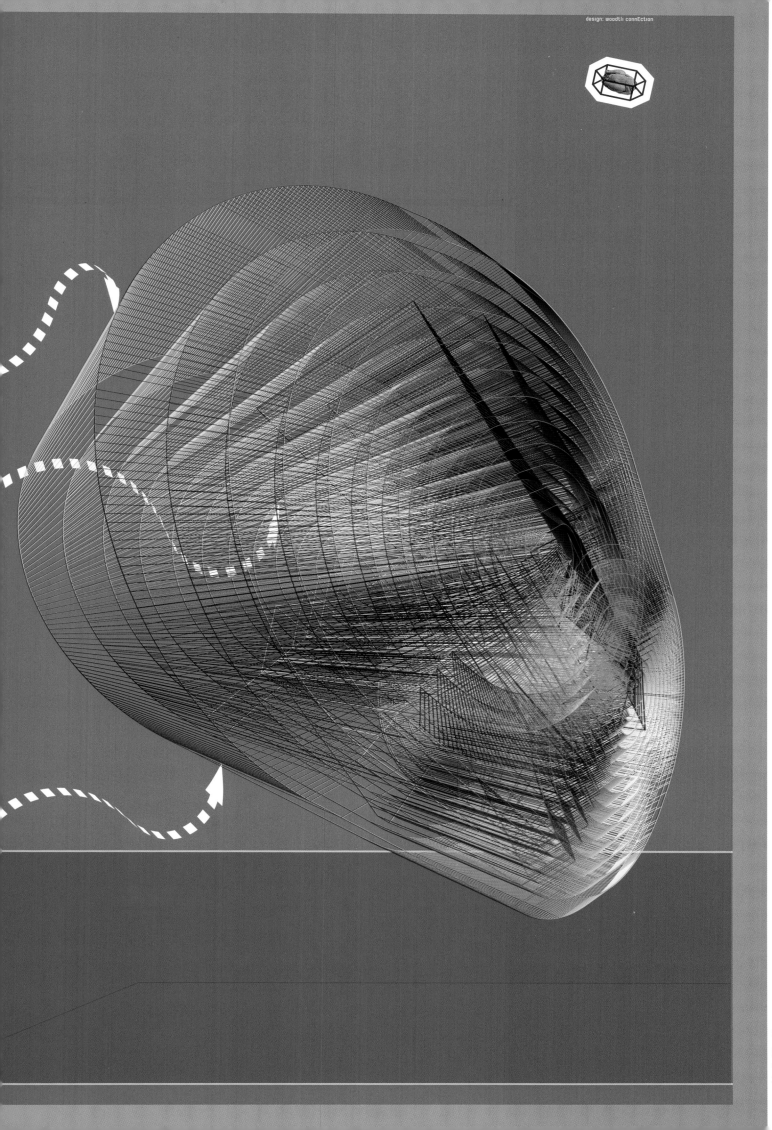

Martin Woodtli
"Set Connection" folder for a gallery event
IKUR
March 1999, Switzerland

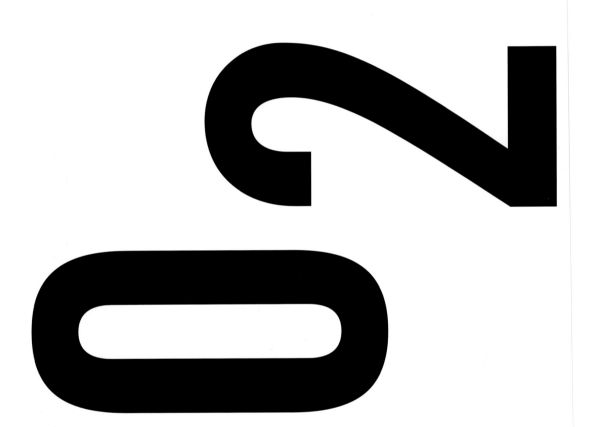

Martin Woodtli
"Dewil's Guest and Cave's Loverman" flyers for an art gallery
Stadtgalerie, Bern
January 2000, Swizterland

COLLECTION

ZAC 99

Laurent Fetis
"Propaganda"
Logo for a fashion hairdressing salon
1999

Laurent Fetis
"Zac 99"
Catalogue cover
Musee d'art moderne de la ville de Paris
1999, France

Laurent Fetis
"Collection" sleeve design
Escalator Records
2000, Japan

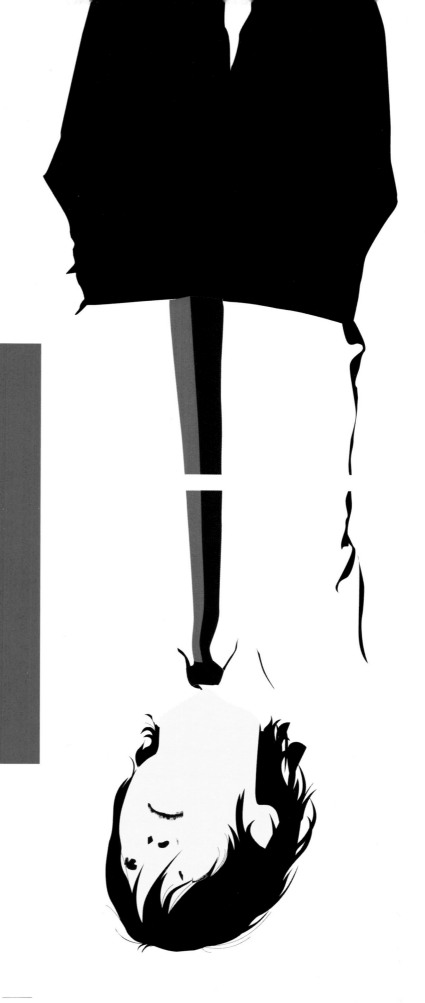

Laurent Fetis
"You will love me" sleeve design
Trattoria Records
2000, Japan
General visual for Hideki Kaji's album.

Laurent Fetis
"Blue in Green" sleeve design for Southern All Stars
JVC/Victor
2001, Japan

Laurent Fetis
"Bless"
April 2001, Japan
Fashion insert for Studio Voice magazine.

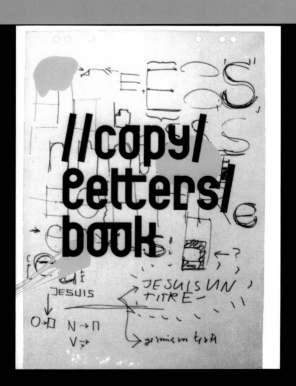

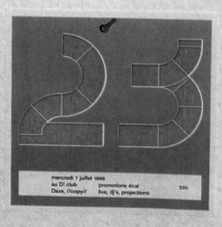

//copy/letters, Laurence Jaccottet, Gregor Schönborn, Niels
Wehrspann
//copy/letters book
Summer 2000, Switzerland
Part font catalogue, part personal manifesto, this book was
designed as a low-budget, non-design project.

//copy/letters, Laurence Jaccottet, Gregor Schönborn, Niels
Wehrspann
//copy/letters book
Summer 2000, Switzerland

MUFFLERS
BRAKES
SHOCKS
STRUTS
C.V. JOINTS
MOST CREDIT CARDS ACCEPTED
212/477-1466
FOREIGN & DOMESTIC
Brake Sale!
CONTENT
SKEP ICISM IS A IR E

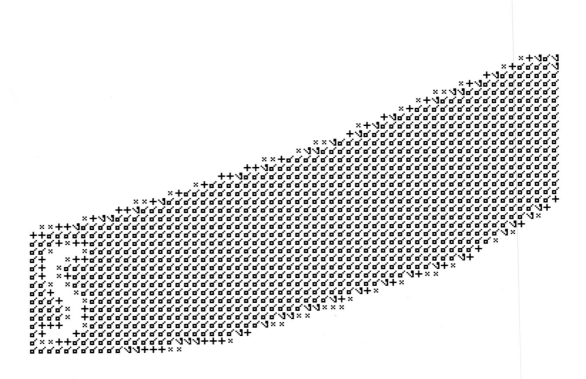

Delaware
Sex Pistols
Original Version "Never Mind The Bollocks"/Sex Pistols/Jamie Reid
1977
2000, Japan
Designed for Delaware's fourth album "Artoon"

Delaware
Mona Lisa
Original Version "MONA Lisa"/Leonald da Vinch 1503-1506
2000, Japan
Designed for Delaware's fourth album "Artoon"

Delaware
Gas Station (detail)
1999, Japan
Designed for Delaware's live show.

Delaware
Gas Station
1999, Japan
Designed for Delaware's live show.

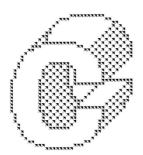

LINO SCRIPT
48PT_REGULAR
OUTLINE FONT(TYPE1)

i_MODE
34PT
LOGO_OF_i_MODE

E
EUROSTILE
48PT_EXTENDED_TWO
OUTLINE FONT(TYPE1)

i_MODE
34PT
LOGO_OF_i_MODE

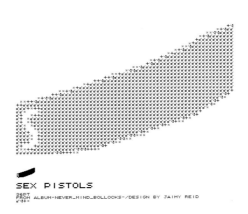

SEX PISTOLS
36PT
FROM ALBUM"NEVER_MIND_BOLLOCKS"/DESIGN BY JAIMY REID

ALAMED
24PT
BITMAP_FONT

LINO SCRIPT
48PT_REGULAR
OUTLINE FONT(TYPE1)

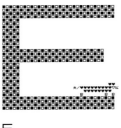

E
EUROSTILE
48PT_EXTENDED_TWO
OUTLINE FONT(TYPE1)

T
TIMES
48PT_ROMAN
OUTLINE FONT(TYPE1)
TIMESHONY

T
TIMES
48PT_ROMAN
OUTLINE FONT(TYPE1)
TIMESHONY

E
EUROSTILE
48PT_EXTENDED_TWO
OUTLINE FONT(TYPE1)

N
NEWS GOTHIC
12PT-BOLD-OBLIQUE
OUTLINE FONT(TYPE1)
NG!

T
TIMES
48PT-ROMAN
OUTLINE FONT (TYPE1)
♪TIMESHONY

f
FUTURA
48PT-EXTRA-BOLD
OUTLINE FONT(TYPE1)
NO·!

◊
OCRA
12PT-REGULAR
OUTLINE FONT (TYPE1)
§GO

U
UNIVERSE
48PT-75-BLACK-OBLIQUE
OUTLINE FONT(TYPE1)
●%

A
RUBBER SOUL
36PT
FROM BEATLES ALBUM-"RUBBER_SOUL"
JOHN♥PAUL♥GER!♪♡

B
WOODSTOCK
48PT
BITMAP FONT

◊
OCRA
12PT-REGULAR
OUTLINE FONT (TYPE1)
§GO

R
RUBBER SOUL
36PT
FROM BEATLES ALBUM-"RUBBER_SOUL"
JOHN♥PAUL♥GER!♪♡

Delaware
Alphabetoon
2000, Japan
Designed for Delaware's fourth album "Artoon".

FACTOR 2

NOT DREADED RISK. VOLUNTARY

LAETRILE · LAETRILE · LAETRILE · LAETRILE · LAETRILE

MICROWAVE OVENS · MICROWAVE

WATER FLUORIDATION · WATER FLUORIDATION

SACCHARIN · SACCHARIN · SACCHARIN · SACCHARIN

HEXACHLOROPHENE · HEXACHLOROPHENE

NITRITES · NITRITES · NITRITES · NITRITES · NITRITES · NITRITES

POLYVINYL CHLORIDE · POLYVINYL CHLORIDE · POLYVINYL CHLORIDE · POLYVINYL CHLORIDE · POLYVINYL

NITROGEN FERTILIZERS

MIREX · MIREX · MIREX · MIREX · MIREX

COAL TAR HAIRDYES · COAL TAR HAIRDYES · COAL TAR HAIRDYES

ORAL CONTRACEPTIVES · ORAL CONTRACEPTIVES

VALIUM · VALIUM · VALIUM · VALIUM · VALIUM · VALIUM

IVD · IVD · IVD · IVD · IVD · IVD

DARVON · DARVON · DARVON

DIAGNOSTIC X-RAYS · DIAGNOSTIC X-RAYS · DIAGNOSTIC X-RAYS

ANTIBIOTICS · ANTIBIOTICS · ANTIBIOTICS · ANTIBIOTICS

INSUL

RUBBER MFG. · RUBBER MFG. · RUBBER MFG. · RUBBER MFG.

CAFFEINE · CAFFEINE · CAFFEINE

ASPIRIN · ASPIRIN · ASPIRIN

AUTO LEAD · AUTO LEAD · AUTO LEAD · AUTO LEAD · AUTO LEAD · AUTO LEAD

MERCUR

LEAD PAINT · LEAD PAINT · LEAD PAINT · LEAD PAINT · LEAD PAINT · LEAD PAINT · LEAD PAINT

VACCINES · VACCINES · VACCINES · VACCINES · VACCINES

AUTO EXH

SKATEBOARDS · SKATEBOARDS

SMOKING (DISEASE) · SMOKING (DISEASE) · SMOKING (DISEASE)

POWER MOWERS · POWER MOWERS

SNOWMOBILES · SNOWMOBILES · SNOWMOBILES · SNOWMOBILES

TRAMPOLINES · TRAMPOLINES

TRACTORS · TRACTORS · TRACTORS

ALCOHOL · ALCOHOL · ALCOHOL · ALCOHOL · ALCOHOL

CHAINSAWS · CHAINSAWS · CHAINSAWS

HOME SWIMMING · ELECTRIC WIRES (FIRES)

ELEVATORS · ELEVATORS · ELEVATORS · ELEVATORS

SMOKING (FIRES) · SMOKING (FIRES) · SMOKING (FIRES)

MOTORCYCLES · MOTORCYCLES

DREADED RISK. INVOLUNTARY

FACTOR 1

DNA TECHNOLOGY

SST

DES

TRICHLOROETHYLENE

PESTICIDES

DDT

FOSSIL FUELS

COAL BURNING (POLLUTION)

2,4,5-T

PCB'S

URANIUM MINING

SATELLITE CRASHES

RADIOACTIVE WASTE

NUCLEAR REACTOR ACCIDENTS

NUCLEAR WEAPONS FALLOUT

LNG-STORAGE & TRANSPORT

NERVE GAS ACCIDENTS

D-CON

SKYSCRAPER FIRES

LARGE DAMS

COAL MINING (DISEASE)

GENERAL AVIATION

HIGH CONSTRU

COAL MINING ACCIDENTS

NUCLEAR WEAPONS (WAR)

Lust

Risk perception carpet for InfoArcadia exhibition

Ronald van Tienhoven/Maarten de Reus/Stroom HCBK

January 2000, The Netherlands

InfoArcadia was an exhibition about data and information and the manner in which they are visualised. The carpet was an interpretation of the information that Paul Slovic gathered in 1988 on people's perceptions of risks. 81 risks were chosen out of more than 40,000 answers, and a way was needed to visualise the x-y matrix onto which the risks were mapped.

RISK PERCEPTIONS

IMPORTANCE OF ACCIDENTS
AS SIGNALS TO SOCIETY

UNIMPORTANT   IMPORTANT

DESIRE FOR STRICT REGULATION
TO REDUCE RISK

NOT STRICT   VERY STRICT

RESEARCH AND COGNITIVE MAP
BY PAUL SLOVIC (1987)
THE ORIGINAL VERSION OF THIS MAP WAS
DERIVED FROM MORE THAN 40,000 JUDGMENTS
(81 HAZARDS X 34 JUDGES X 15 JUDGES PER HAZARD)
REDRAWN BY LUST (2000)

IMMEDIATE EFFECT

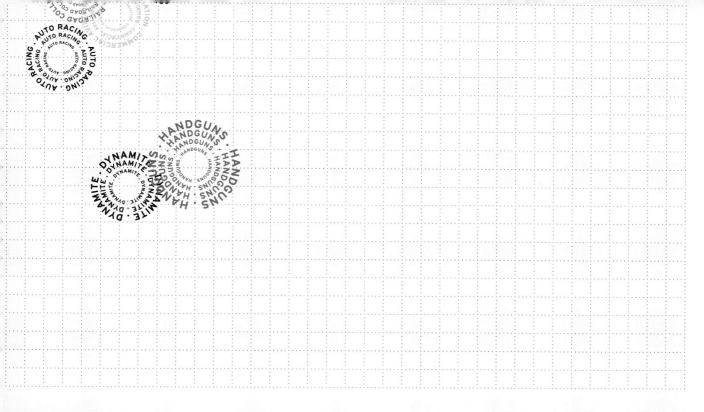

KNOWN RISK.

Lust
StereoType, DaaRom CD-Rom
MacWorld NL/TYP
June 1998, The Netherlands
An alternative "type specimen" sheet demonstrating a new
monospaced Lust-font, designed for computer screens.

Lust, in collaboration with Design Arbeid
Paradiso V.I.P. cards
Paradiso club
December 2000, The Netherlands
A program on a business card sized CD-Rom, illustrated with a per-
sonalised image; available to VIP members of the Paradiso club.
The program allows users to play around with a computer keyboard
combining graphics and sounds. A Flash-version can be found at
www.lust.nl (on the "Parasite" page).

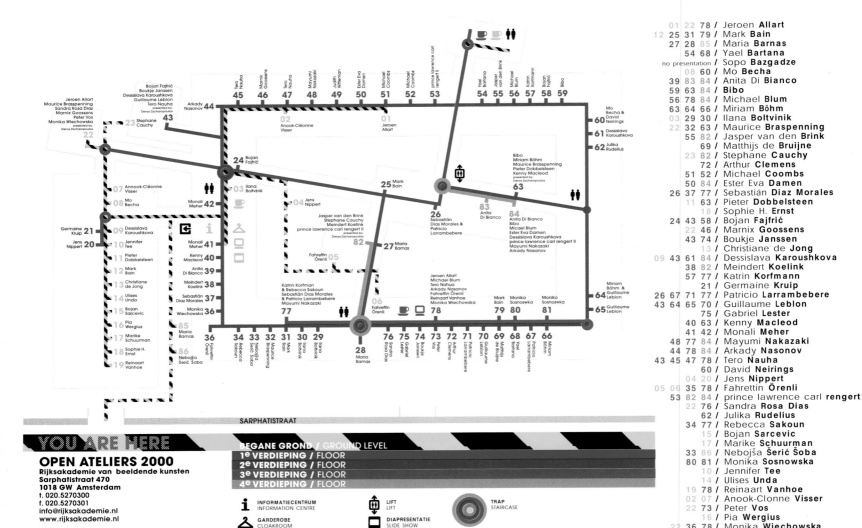

SARPHATISTRAAT

YOU ARE HERE

OPEN ATELIERS 2000
Rijksakademie van beeldende kunsten
Sarphatistraat 470
1018 GW Amsterdam
t. 020.5270300
f. 020.5270301
info@rijksakademie.nl
www.rijksakademie.nl

BEGANE GROND / GROUND LEVEL
1e VERDIEPING / FLOOR
2e VERDIEPING / FLOOR
3e VERDIEPING / FLOOR
4e VERDIEPING / FLOOR

INFORMATIECENTRUM / INFORMATION CENTRE
GARDEROBE / CLOAKROOM
TOILET / TOILET
KOFFIE, FRIS, BROODJES, ETC. / COFFEE, SOFTDRINKS, SANDWICHES, ETC.
LIFT / LIFT
DIAPRESENTATIE / SLIDE SHOW
WEBSITE / WEBSITE
INGANG / ENTRANCE
TRAP / STAIRCASE
BUITEN / OUTSIDE

Lust
"You Are Here: Open Ateliers 2000", logo, map, exhibition signage
Rijksakademie van de Beeldende, Amsterdam
October 2000, The Netherlands

The complicated floor plan of the Rijksakademie required a
simplifying signage system for the Open Ateliers. Various coloured
tapes and patterns, applied to the floor were used to designate
areas in a five-storey complex. This led to the design of the map,
which resembled a subway system, i.e., one colour = one line = one
floor, one number = one stop = one atelier. Yellow and black tape
was used as the main image for the print work, in reference to the
signage system, and for easy recognition.

Molecule, Stuart Bailey and Ruth Blacksell
Everything magazine 3.3, cover designed with Paul Elliman
Summer 2000, UK

DE BEST VERZORGDE BOEKEN 1999
THE BEST

...HE BEST ...OOK ...ESIGNS

...oor De huid van het geheugen door Jan Wolkers
...by Skinscapes by Jan Wolkers

9 789074 336628

Molecule, Stuart Bailey and Christine Alberts
Best Designed Books catalogue 1999
Stedelijk Museum, Amsterdam
Spring 2000, The Netherlands
Designed in reaction to exhibition catalogues that emphasise the
graphic design content over the work documented. This catalogue
lists all the details of the winning publications, including the
personnel (designers, printers, binders etc.) and their tools
(typefaces, paper, presses etc.), all wrapped in a no-nonsense
white paper cover.

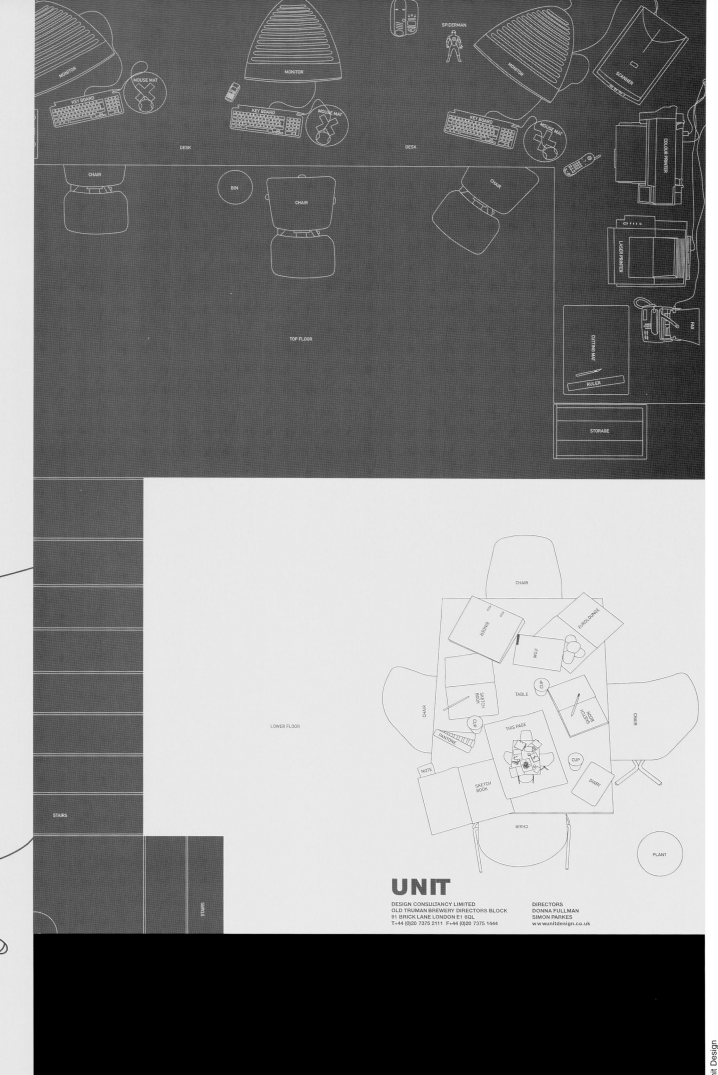

UNIT

DESIGN CONSULTANCY LIMITED
OLD TRUMAN BREWERY DIRECTORS BLOCK
91 BRICK LANE LONDON E1 6QL
T+44 (0)20 7375 2111 F+44 (0)20 7375 1444

DIRECTORS
DONNA FULLMAN
SIMON PARKES
www.unitdesign.co.uk

Unit Design
Self-promotional booklet
October 2000, UK

www.and-or.org

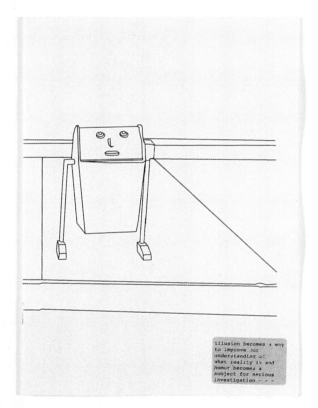

Seeing is Believing
by Vik Muniz, Charles Stainback

Best described as an artist who uses a camera, Vik Muniz blurs the
lines between painting, sculpture, and photography. He has made a
number of different series of photographs in which he constructs
images--often portraits--out of materials such as sugar, chocolate
syrup, and thread. In another series, he drew famous images (using
his aforementioned nontraditional media), like the photograph of
Neil Armstrong on the moon, from memory. Muniz plays freely in the
field of representation. And through his work, viewers witness the
complicated separation between a real image that seems definitely
to exist somewhere, and the means by which Muniz achieves a representation of that image--first re-creating it, then making a photograph. He writes that "illusion becomes a way to improve our
understanding of what reality is and humor becomes a subject for
serious investigation." By setting up images that aim to unsettle
viewers' perceptual faculties as a way of expanding understanding,
and stimulating discovery, Muniz takes part in a trend in image-
making that includes artistssuch as Gerhard Richter, Richard
Artschwager, and Thomas Demand.
Published alongside his solo exhibition at the International
Center of Photography in New York, Seeing Is Believing is the
first monograph on Vik Muniz. The reproduction of the images on
heavy, creamy paper is of exceptional quality, indicative of its
publisher, Arena Editions. And the book includes two essays, one
by Charles Ashley Stainback and the other by Mark Alice Durant, as
well as a dialogue between Muniz and Stainback.

http://www.amazon.com/exec/obidos/ASIN/1892041006/qid=969964018/sr=
1-4/002-3877018-9315232

introduction

Aalex Bettler
"and-or" booklets
Diploma project, École Cantonale d'Art de Lausanne
October 2000, Switzerland

Three booklets or "fanzines" of related images and texts make
observations on and connections between the ordinary, everyday
things that surround us. So as to reflect this, the design of the book
is simple and cheap, for ease of production and distribution.

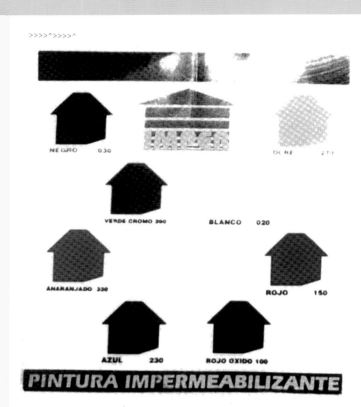

NEGRO 030

OCRE 270

VERDE CROMO 290

BLANCO 020

ANARANJADO 330

ROJO 150

AZUL 230

ROJO OXIDO 100

PINTURA IMPERMEABILIZANTE

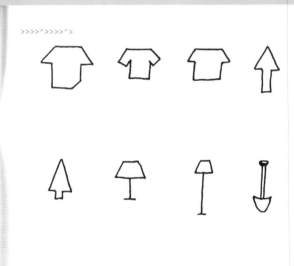

```
...
> a 3d house
> a t-shirt
> a house
> an arrow
> a pine tree
> a small lamp
> a lamp
> a paddle
...
```

>>>

Courier New

>>>

Arial Black

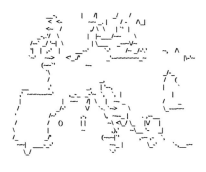

TIMES NEW ROMAN

TheMix SC-Caps

BIRTHDAY CARD

Before giving card, tick box or specify which birthday is being celebrated.

- ☐ Eighteenth
- ☐ Twenty-first
- ☐ Fortieth
- ☐ Fiftieth
- ☐ Hundredth
- ☐ Other*

*Please specify _____ —

↑ **THIS WAY UP** | ☂ | ⬆ By Hand | 🗑 | ♻

GREETING CARD

Using a red pen delete all descriptions that are not relevant to the recipient of the card.

- Mum
- Dad
- Daughter
- Son
- Sister
- Brother
- Grandma
- Grandad
- Grand Daughter
- Grand Son
- Aunt
- Uncle
- Cousin
- Nephew

- Niece
- Twin
- Girlfriend
- Boyfriend
- Wife
- Husband
- Friend
- Lover
- Enemy
- Stranger
- Teacher
- Boss
- Neighbour
- Other*

*Please specify _____ — ↑

CUSTOM CARD

Please write or draw a personal message for the card's recipient in the space below.

To	From
....	....

↑ | ☂ | ⬆ By Hand | 🗑 | ♻

LATE CARD

Write an excuse or apology in no more than fifty words to explain why this card is late.

—
_____
_____
_____
_____
_____
_____

I promise that I will try harder next time to make sure your card arrives on time!

Signed	Date
....	....

CHAIN CARD

This chain card can be sent and received a maximum of five times.

Please complete a section below:

1. Name _____ Occasion _____

2. Name _____ Occasion _____

3. Name _____ Occasion _____

4. Name _____ Occasion _____

5. Name _____ Occasion _____

Please be responsible when writing on the inside of this card and allow space for other senders to write a short message.	Do not throw the card away until it has been sent five times.

USE A NEW ENVELOPE EACH TIME THE CARD IS SENT! 🗑

LUCKY CARD

Give somebody a chance in a million. Affix a National Lottery Scratch Card inside.

Please note that this is a lucky card and that any winnings must be divided equally between:

1. Card's recipient [_____]

2. Card's sender [_____]

Recipients' and senders' names must be written in full using capital letters in red pen. Any deviation will render the card invalid and will result in the recipient having full rights to the winnings.

Responsibility cannot be accepted for the loss of this card and lottery ticket.

INSTANT CASH PRIZES TO BE WON, GOOD LUCK! ↑

Eatock Family Composite Christmas Tree

Merry Christmas 1999 / Happy New Year 2000

Father   Mother

Son   Daughter

The Composite Christmas Tree depicted on the front of the card has been created by overlaying the four drawings shown above. Each drawing is printed in a 25% tint of black. When two lines overlap, the density increases to 50%; when three lines overlap the density increases to 75%; and when all four lines overlap, the area becomes 100% black.

25% Black   50% Black   75% Black   100% Black

Daniel Eatock/Foundation 33
Utilitarian greetings cards
1998, UK
Each card is embellished with the motto "Say YES to fun and function and NO to seductive imagery and colour!".

Danial Eatock/Foundation 33
Family Christmas card
1999, UK
The image is made up of a composite of Christmas trees, each drawn by a different member of the Eatock family. The drawings were printed in a 25% tint to produce a 100% tint where all four drawings overlap.

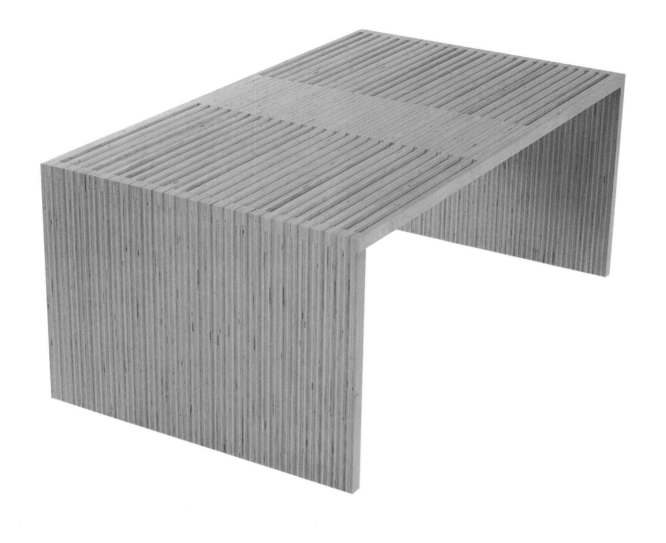

Foundation 33/Eatock/Solhaug
Multi-ply tables
2000, UK

Tables constructed by laminating plywood strips that were cut by computer to stringent instructions designed to maximise the usage of a standard 4x8-feet sheet so as to eliminate waste.

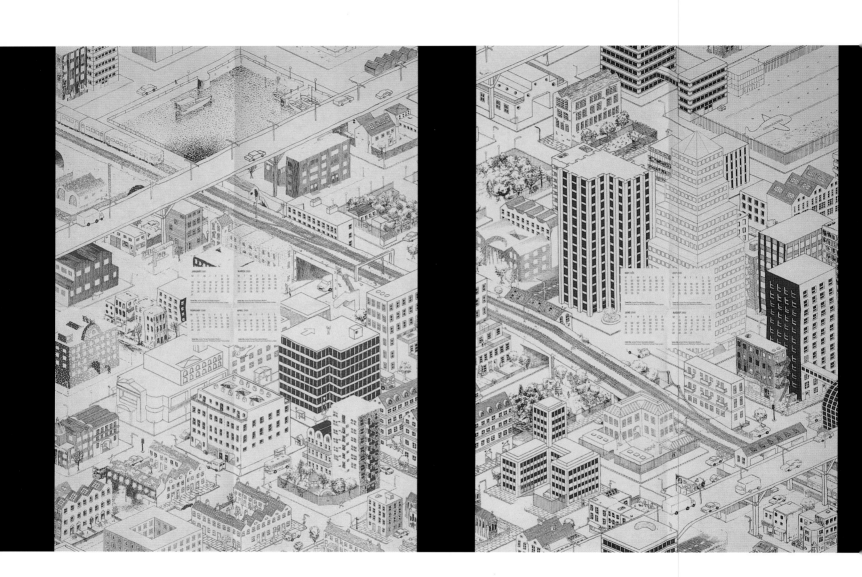

Secondary Modern
Calender
2000, UK

Annual collaboration to produce promotional item; for the year 2000
James Pyman made a large-scale cityscape drawing that filled the
three-sheet format.

ARTWORDSBO
OKSHOPQRST
UVWXYZ
abcontemporar
yvisualculture
1234567890
&$-/...;;?!*""''

ARTWORDS BOOKSHOP, 65a Rivington Street, Shoreditch, London EC2A 3QQ
Telephone: (0)20 7729 2000; Fax: (0)20 7729 4400; shop@artwords.co.uk; www.artwords.co.uk

Secondary Modern
Bookshop identity on carrier bag
Artwords Bookshop
2000, UK
Part of an identity for a specialist retailer in London.

Zoë Hope Engraving

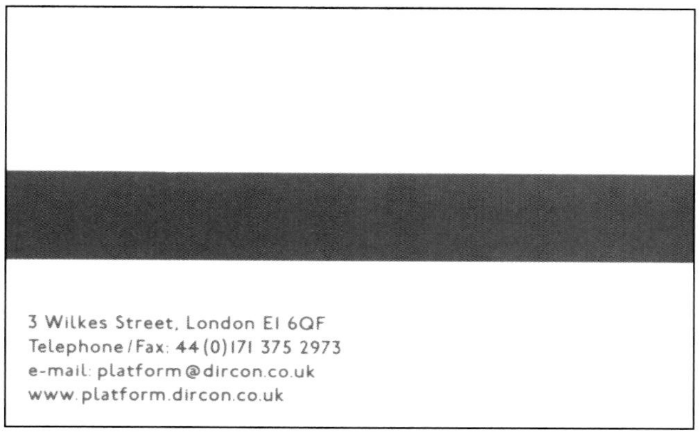

3 Wilkes Street, London EI 6QF
Telephone/Fax: 44 (0)171 375 2973
e-mail: platform@dircon.co.uk
www.platform.dircon.co.uk

Platform

Secondary Modern
Identity and stationery for a designer
Zoe Hope
2000, UK

Secondary Modern
Identity for a project space
Platform
1999, UK

MP

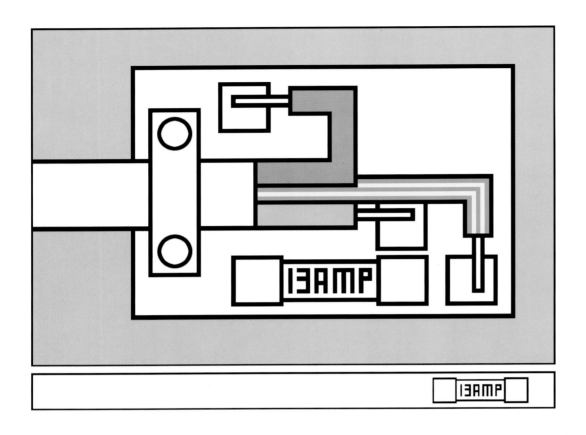

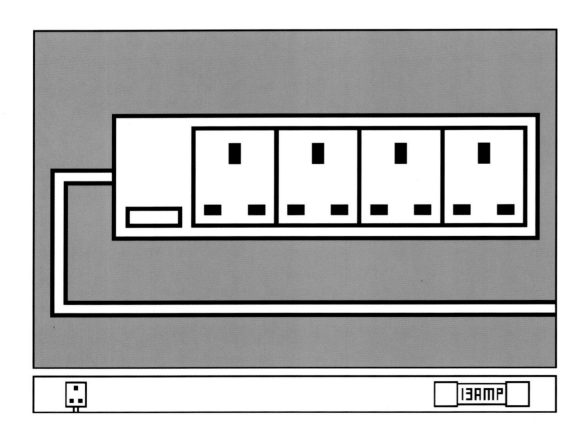

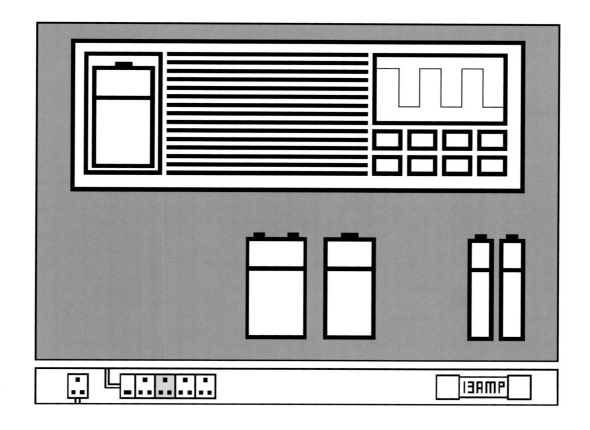

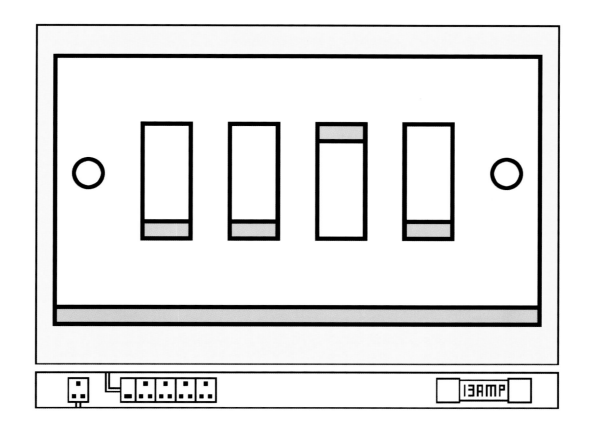

Friendchip
website www.13amp.tv
13amp Records
June 2001, UK

A series of interactive "sound toys", based on the theme of
electricity for a newly-launched record label. The site is intended to
evolve over several months so as to build interest.

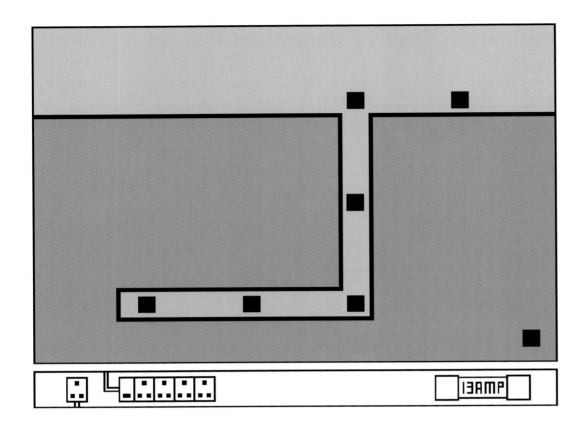

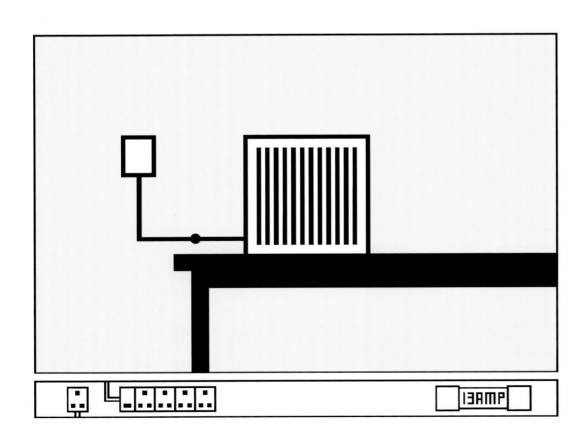

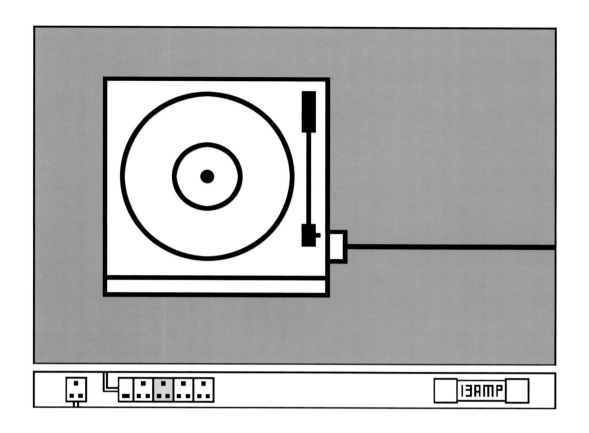

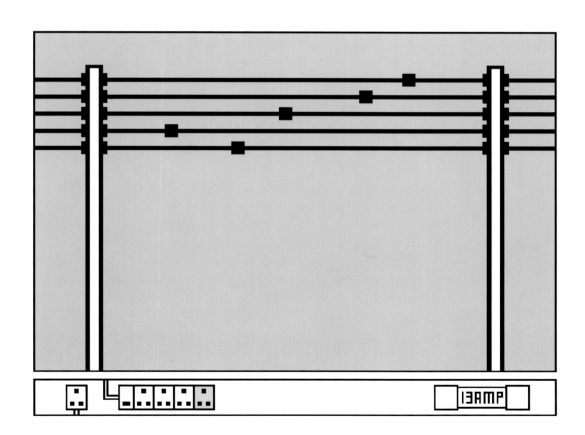

Friendchip
website www.13amp.tv
13amp Records
June 2001, UK

THE STEALING EYEBALLS JAZZ MIT PFIFF.

REALA SE/SUI

ANNOUNCEMENT !
REALA LECTURE + CONCERT AT K/HAUS VIENNA
---> FEATURING SECONDO / DRECK + HMS / RE>RE>RE>

12 MAI 2001 (SAT) --> 16 : 00 K/HAUS

LIVE

EURO

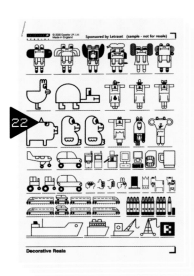

Decorative Reala

Pez Regular 48pt.   Complete digital set available from www.linoto.com

Biff 36pt.   Complete digital set available from www.linoto.com

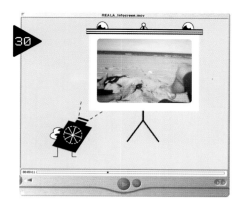

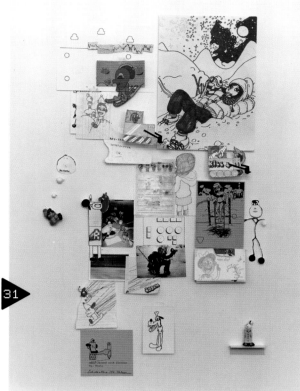

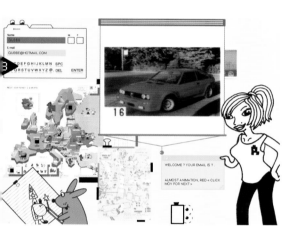

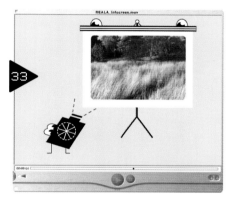

TEALING EYEBALLS JAZZ

1 CONTRIBUTION TO 'DER STANDARD' (AUSTRIAN NEWSPAPER) FOR STEALING EYEBALLS EXHIBITION, VIENNA, 2001
2 CONTRIBUTION TO 'DE:BUG' MAGAZINE (D) FOR STEALING EYEBALLS, VIENNA, 2001
3 INTERACTIVE EXHIBITION PIECE FOR STEALING EYEBALLS, VIENNA, 2001
4 REALA LECTURE + SECONDO/RE:RE:RE: CONCERT ANNOUNCEMENT-POSTER FOR STEALING EYEBALLS, 2001
5 ANIMATION FOR THE VIENNESE UNDERGROUND SYSTEM, STEALING EYBALLS, VIENNA, , 2001
6 SCANIA
7 DECORATIVE REALA, COMING SOON TO WWW.LINETOGÜBBE.COM
8 DRK CD 01, 2000

HIS SPREAD

2 DECORATIVE REALA, LETRASET SHEET, SPOSORED BY LETRASET/ESSELTE, 2000
3 PEZ, LETRASET SHEET, SPOSORED BY LETRASET/ESSELTE, 2000
4 BIFF, LETRASET SHEET, SPOSORED BY LETRASET/ESSELTE, 2000
5 BALLET ACADEMY OF STOCKHOLM, MULTIPURPOSE-ON-TOUR-1-CORNER PER PERFORMANCE-POSTER/BOOKLET, 2001
6 20 YEAR ANNIVERSARY INVITATION CARD FOR MEKANO, FILM COMPANY, SWEDEN
7 ROYAL, ROYAL, DUSTDRAWING + POSTCARD (CHRS ALX)
8 INTERACTIVE EXHIBITION PIECE, STEALING EYEBALLS, VIENNA, 2001
9 UNDMITAUCH, LETRASET SHEET, SPOSORED BY LETRASET/ESSELTE, 2000
0 ANIMATION FOR INFOSCREEN, STEALING EYEBALLS, VIENNA, 2000
1 MENU CARD, LYDMAR HOTEL, STOCKHOLM, 2001
2 RE:RE:RE:, 10TH AWARDWINNING COMPILATION CD
3 ANIMATION FOR INFOSCREEN, STEALING EYEBALLS, VIENNA, 2000

Reala
2001, Switzerland/Sweden

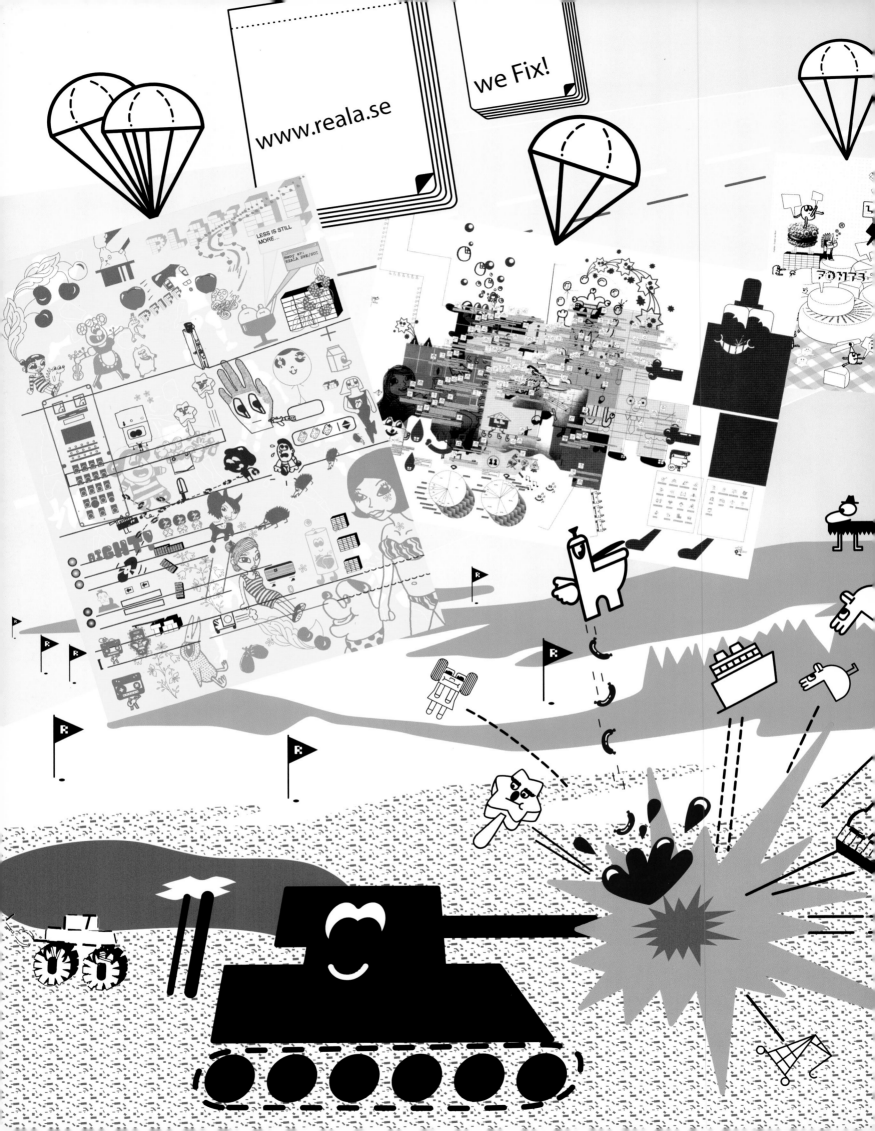

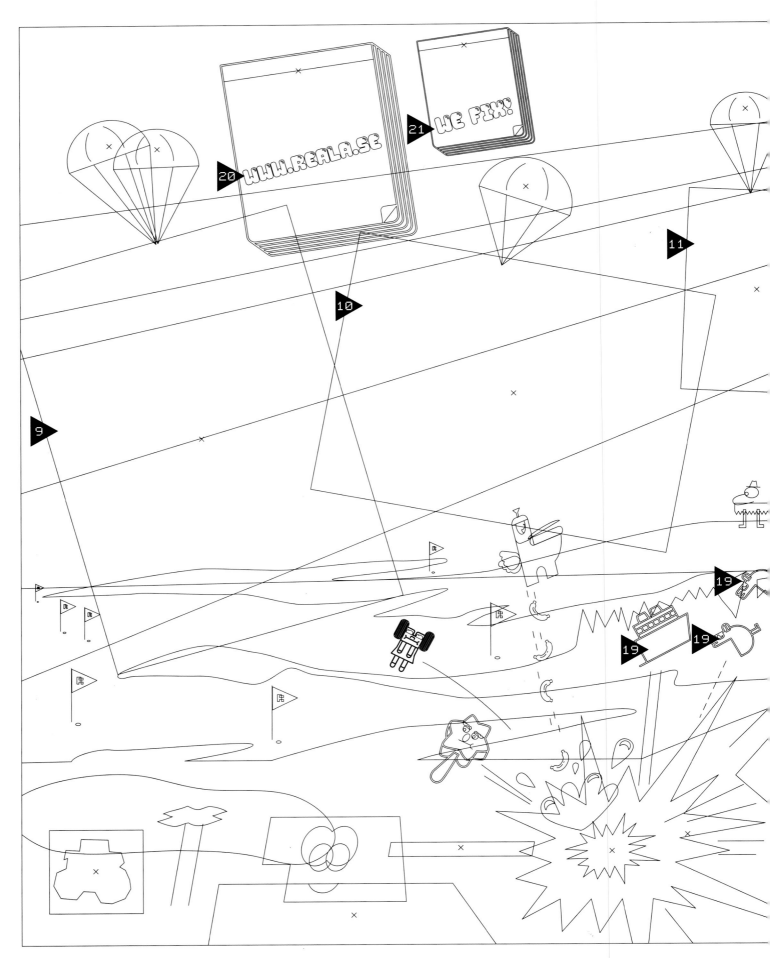

09 MENU-CARD, LYDMAR HOTEL, STOCKHOLM, 2001   10 MIGROS KULTURBEUTEL, SPONSORING CHART, SWITZERLAND, 200
11 ADVERT FOR LINETO FONT FOUNDRY, SWITZERLAND, 2000   12 MARKETING FOR DEUTSCH-ISRAELISCHE FREUNDSCHA
13 DRK/RAL COMPIL. ON DRECK RECORDS FEATURING SECONDO, RE:RE:RE: & LRNT, 2000

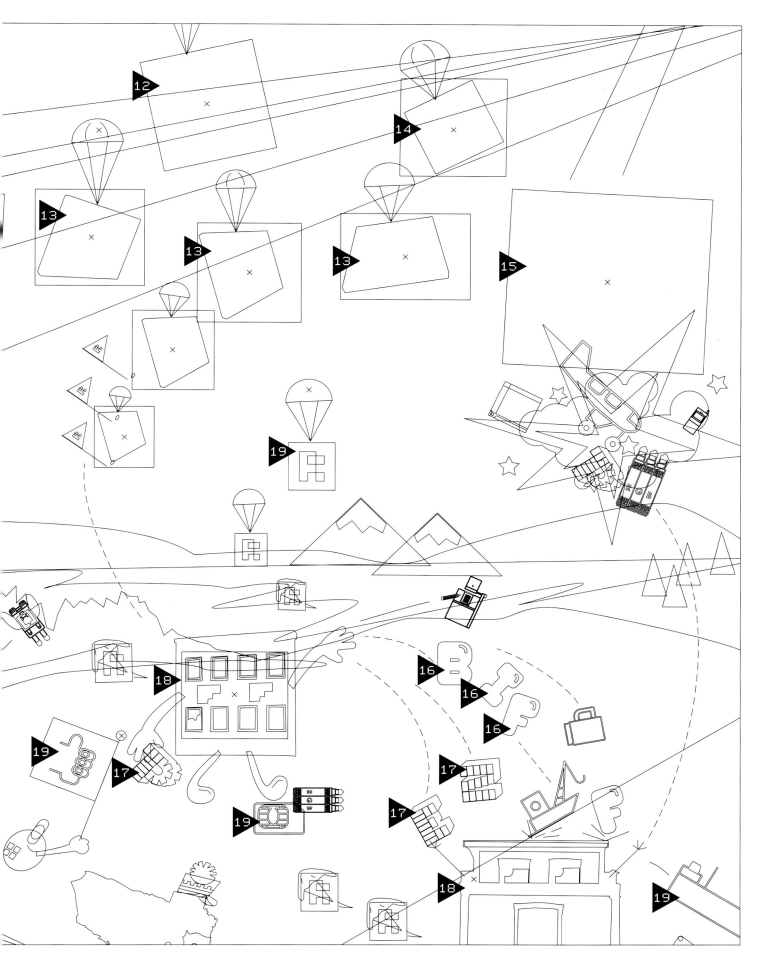

RE:RE:RE: 10TH AWARD-WINNING COMPILATION 15 ANIMATION FOR INFOSCREEN, STEALING EYEBALLS, VIENNA, 2001
BIFF-FONT, AVAILABLE FROM WWW.LINETO.COM 17 PEZ-FONT, AVAILABLE FROM WWW.LINETO.COM 18 GÜBBE, GÜBBE
DECORATIVE REALA, COMING SOON TO WWW.LINETO.COM 20 WE RECOMMEND 21 TRUE!

Reala
2001, Switzerland/Sweden

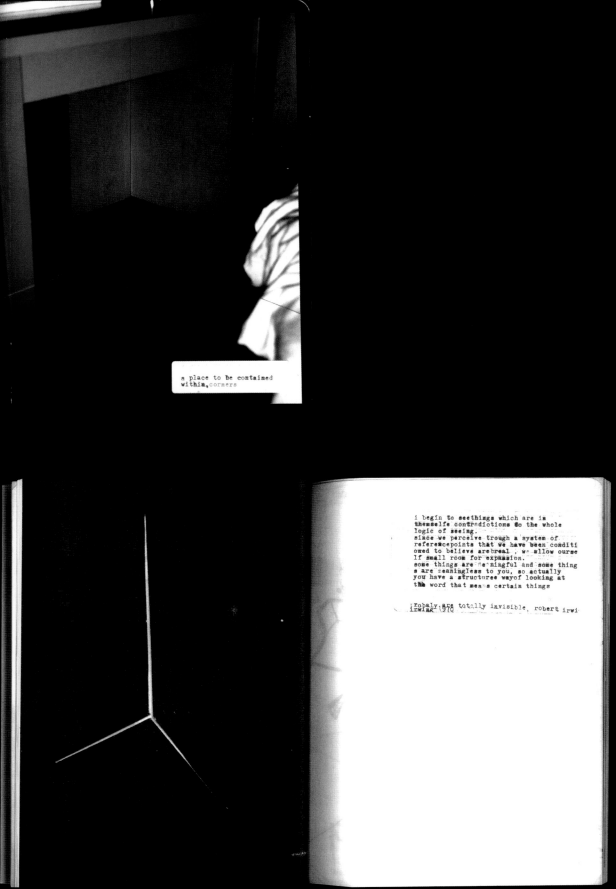

a place to be contained
within,corners

i begin to seethings which are in
themselfe contradictions to the whole
logic of seeing.
since we perceive trough a system of
referencepoints that we have been conditi
oned to believe arebreal , we allow ourse
lf small room for expansion.
some things are meaningful and some thing
s are meaningless to you, so actually
you have a structuree wayof looking at
the word that means certain things

[robaly are totally invisible, robert irwi
irwin 1970

mdf, wood laminate, rosewood
70 × 35 × 35 cm

Carolin Kurz
A place to be contained within, corners
Martin Gamper
2001, UK
A book designed in collaboration with product designer Martin
Gamper to illustrate his furniture designs within the context of
existing corners.

AMBIT: Poems, Short Stories, Pictures. 17 Priory Gardens, London N6 5QY www.ambit.co.uk

STOP THE
F
BUS NOW!

WOODLEY RESIDENTS AGAINST ROUTE F BUSES

STOP THE
F
BUS NOW!

WOODLEY RESIDENTS AGAINST ROUTE F BUSES

John Morgan
"Stop the F Bus" poster campaign
Woodley F bus residents campaign
Summer 2000, UK
A campaign to stop old "F" buses that are heavy polluters. Graffiti
on one of the posters makes the point more explicitly.

John Morgan
Poster for Ambit magazine
Ambit
2000/2001, UK

spelling. Many of today's Western "phonetic" languages, with their irrational spelling, are far from ideal phonetic languages. Phonetic systems don't use silent letters, all the letters are pronounced. A more true phonetic writing is used by the Eastern-European languages. The Slavic languages use more characters in order to avoid ambiguities in spelling. The Slovak language, for example, uses up to 44 signs, nearly twice as many as English. Although written Slovak is closely linked to its pronunciation, Slovak too has a significant number of exceptions in writing. A "real" phonetic language would probably use even more characters. ¶ I recall a lecture by the French artist Pierre di Sciullo at the FUSE conference in Berlin. A idea

Peter Bilak
Transparency
1997, Bratislava
A book about means of communication and the difficulty of maintaining clarity when form gets in the way of ideas. Readers have the option of viewing pages as type-images, or using the colour transparency to decipher the text.

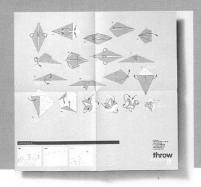

NB Studio
Make your own! Christmas card
1999, UK

The card comprises a sheet of self-adhesive stickers, a red C6
envelope and a blank, but scored, white card, enclosed in a clear
plastic bag. The stickers include all the words and symbols
necessary to create a festive greeting.

NB Studio
Christmas Card
2000, UK

An origami set, branded and packaged as "Throw It ©"; the pack
contains everything needed to make an origami snowball, including
ten sheets of paper, folding instructions and an operating guide.

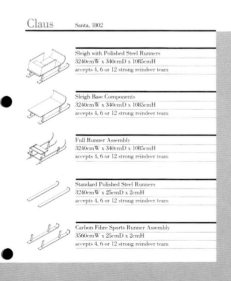

NB Studio
Knoll Christmas card
Knoll UK
1998, UK

A spoof of the information cards a furniture company posts to clients so as to update specification books; the featured "St. Nicholas Range" of sledges has carbon fibre runners and reindeer-hide seats. The adapted Knoll logo hints at the card's true nature.

A type face is an integral part of a corporate identity. It supports the identity by adding both personality and functionality.
Dalton Maag specialises in designing logo types and corporate type faces.

A type face is an integral part of a corporate identity. It supports the identity by adding both personality and functionality.
Dalton Maag specialises in designing logo types and corporate type faces.

Eine Schrift ist ein wesentlicher Bestandteil eines Firmenerscheinungsbildes. Sie unterstützt die Identität durch Anmutung, persönlichen Ausdruck und Funktionalität.
Dalton Maag haben sich auf die Gestaltung von Logo- und Firmenschriften spezialisiert.

Projects
Projekte

A type face is an integral part of a corporate identity. It supports the identity by adding both personality and functionality.
Dalton Maag specialises in designing logo types and corporate type faces.

Eine Schrift ist ein wesentlicher Bestandteil eines Firmenerscheinungsbildes. Sie unterstützt die Identität durch Anmutung, persönlichen Ausdruck und Funktionalität.
Dalton Maag haben sich auf die Gestaltung von Logo- und Firmenschriften spezialisiert.

Dalton Maag **Unit M2**
245A Coldharbour Lane
London SW9 8RR
T 0044 171 924 0633
F 0044 171 738 6410

Valerie Kiock
Dalton Mag brochure
June 1999, UK
Promotional brochure for a typesetting and design company.

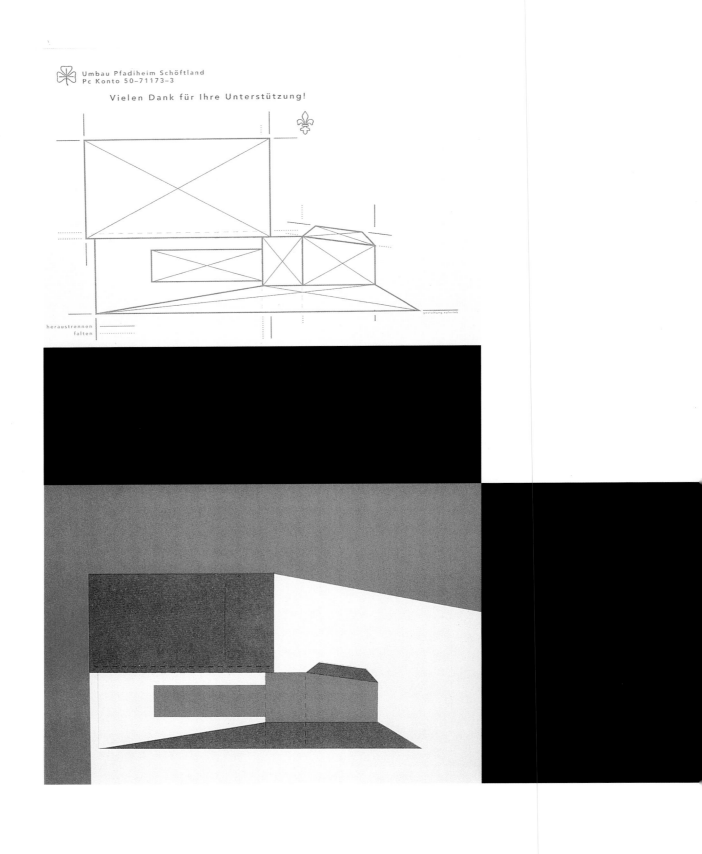

Umbau Pfadiheim Schöftland
Pc Konto 50-71173-3

Vielen Dank für Ihre Unterstützung!

heraustrennen
falten

Valerie Klock
"Schötland" postcard
Jörg Boner
August 1998, Switzerland
A postcard sold to raise funds for the rebuilding of a Boy Scouts'
cottage. A model of the cottage can be constructed from the pre-
scored card.

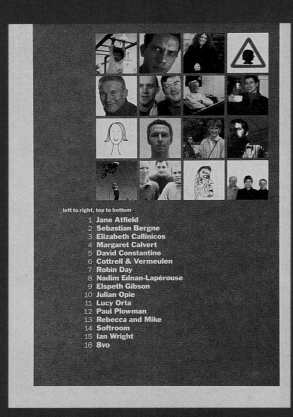

left to right, top to bottom

1 Jane Atfield
2 Sebastian Bergne
3 Elizabeth Callinicos
4 Margaret Calvert
5 David Constantine
6 Cottrell & Vermeulen
7 Robin Day
8 Nadim Ednan-Lapérouse
9 Elspeth Gibson
10 Julian Opie
11 Lucy Orta
12 Paul Plowman
13 Rebecca and Mike
14 Softroom
15 Ian Wright
16 8vo

The British Council cause+effect/16 designers

---

cross his mind that it would be possible to earn a living from it. 'At school I wasn't really very good at art,' he says. 'And at that period people weren't so aware of des̲   If nobody in your family did it, you didn't really know about it.' After leaving school he got a job in an office. 'But I just carried on drawing,' he says. 'I used to draw on the blotting paper at work, make birthday cards and stuff.'

Eventually, a colleague persuaded him to try an evening class in art, and there the teacher suggested he should go to art college. 'She was the first "official" person who said   he remembers.

cross his mind that it would be possible to earn a living from it. 'At school I wasn't really very good at art,' he says. 'And at that period people weren't so aware of d̲esign. If nobody in your family did it, you didn't really know about it.' After leaving school he got a job in an office. 'But I just carried on drawing,' he says. 'I used to draw on the blotting paper at work, make birthday cards and stuff.'

Eventually, a colleague persuaded him to try an evening class in art, and there the teacher suggested he should go to art college. 'She was the first "official" person who said "you   he remembers.

cross his mind that it would be possible to earn a living from it. 'At school I wasn't really very good at art,' he says. 'And at that period people weren't so aware of d̲esign. If nobody in your family did it, you didn't really know about it.' After leaving school he got a job in an office. 'But I just carried on drawing,' he says. 'I used to draw on the blotting paper at work, make birthday cards and stuff.'

Eventually, a colleague persuaded him to try an evening class in art, and there the teacher suggested he should go to art college. 'She was the first "official" person who said "you can do this",' he remembers.

Sans + Baum
"Cause and Effect" exhibition catalogue
The British Council
February 2001, UK

| ACHTERZAAL | **BERMUDA DRIEHOEK** |
| | JAN KEMPENAERS JURRIAAN MOLENAAR KATRINE HJELDE |

| VOORZAAL | *PUBLIEK / PRIVÉ* | *TOO RISKY* | *PERFORMANCE* |
| | YVONNE LE GRAND 17-01 > 01-02 | LISA HOLDEN 07-02 > 22-02 | TOMMY OLSSON |

MET DANK AAN: MONDRIAAN STICHTING, GEMEENTE AMSTERDAM

BEELD / ONTWERP THOMAS BUXÓ *OK*

Thomas Buxó
Flyers
W139, Amsterdam
1998, The Netherlands

GREATWOOD PARK ADJACENT

Ephemeral Congruity Lot

Thomas Buxó
Exhibition catalogue for "Greatwood Park Adjacent" by Alida Logue
Motevideo Time-based Arts, Amsterdam
1999, The Netherlands

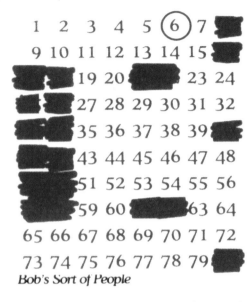

1 2 3 4 5 ⑥ 7 ▮
9 10 11 12 13 14 15 ▮
▮ 19 20 ▮ 23 24
▮ 27 28 29 30 31 32
▮ 35 36 37 38 39 ▮
▮ 43 44 45 46 47 48
▮ 51 52 53 54 55 56
▮ 59 60 ▮ 63 64
65 66 67 68 69 70 71 72
73 74 75 76 77 78 79 ▮

Bob's Sort of People

Time Magazine's "Fraud of the Century"..."Bob's original *Time Control* program has helped many thousands to no longer fear the STARK FIST of REMOVAL."

Bob's Press

Personal Invitation: 3¼ by 5¼"
Dinner: 80 seats
7 courses: *Free*
Wine Arrangement: $10
Water: optional
No other beverages served

Bob's Dining Concept

Choose between:
Dinner or Breakfast:
Saturday March 3rd, Midnight*
Sunday March 4th, 4pm*

*Please allow for an 7 hour lapse in Bob's timing. This being the first application of his patented Dining Concept outside of Texas (Col. 34, Number 6 "Special Handling" applicable to MAMA). Do not spoil your appetite by eating beforehand. Bob says: sleep in, eat late.

Location: Las Palmas
Wilhelminakade 66, Rotterdam
RESERVATIONS ONLY.
RSVP, 1C1S, WYSIWIG.
Call: 316 14737385

mama ⓦ ⓡ | **Werkstad in Las Palmas**

Bob's Local information

$$3 + 1 + 4 + 5 + 1 + 4$$
$$+ 8 + 0 + 7 + 1 + 0 +$$
$$3 + 4 + 4 + 7 + 3 + 4$$
$$+ 6 + 6 + 6 + 1 + 1 +$$
$$3 + 1 + 6 + 1 + 4 + 7$$
$$+ 3 + 7 + 3 + 8 + 5$$
$$= 128, \ 1 + 2 + 8 = 11,$$
$$1 + 1 = 2$$

Bob's Recipe for Success

Bob's seal of approval

Hollerith D-11 card by goodwill

Card 1 (top-left)

beautiful soft light from behind, uber-Deutsch, zeer aardig, scheve bek, confusing green glass. lekker fruitig & bloemig, acidy, definite, paling?, sprookjesachtig. droog en straffelijk, mother's milk at 11 C, meer structuur! niet dun, lekker hard en nat, nice day old spa rood, filling your mouth with 5 cl. heel erg droog, strong, fruity, but very very good, stringy gob to your feet and back, much softer, lovely, I think I would prefer it, winters en koud, maar niet kil, net niet te makkelijk en toch fris, op dit tijdstip een beetje gek, citrus aftertaste, little villages. eyes closed in hammock with a morning sun, Oost-Europa, ochtendhumeur, katerig, hangover, lekkere billen, ronde vormen, Wenen gecombineerd met het Hoge Noorden van Noorwegen, weet je hoe het bij de apen in Blijdorp ruikt?, gras, lammetjes, en lekkere wijven, Charlotte & Blaise, Detroit escalators. een uur of vijf 's middags, NEUK MEER! (en harder), mest, the third sip is best consumed on a ferry, read the label carefully, during a Rotterdam-Amsterdam discussion.

Bob already eight

Bob's choice of wine: Pouilly Fumée 1999   *Bob's seal of approval*

Card 2 (top-right)

kleurnuances, simpel maar sierlijk, geen overbodige fratsen. confronterend aroma, uitgebalanceerd, zwaar achter in de mond, Friday's rubbish before collection. overwegend zacht, incidenteel taai maar overwegend mals, thank Bob it's not too fine or slippery, dun versus gehakt. pure, de combinatie van zout- en zuuraccenten op de zachtheid van het vlees werkt buitengewoon, een verrassende finishing touch, tasty toppings. bewolkte zomerochtend, Old Dirty Bastard, Hannibal. Barcelona 16 p.m., BSE-less, voor de triatleet.

Bob already eight

Bob's Amuse   *Bob's seal of approval*

Card 3 (bottom-left)

shades of green, RGB with the G in particular, geprakt, olijfgroene wolk: simpel maar fijn, rough and rustic, would enjoy it even more in a wooden bowl, looking rather uninteresting, has to do with the colour I think. fresh, lekker scherp in de neus, kruidig, beetje zoet, scherpgroen, very strong, specific indication of the veg, Sunday afternoon with the neighbours. light and wealthy, fresh and simple, 15 groen-gele velden en waterzakjes, stevig, vezelig, als in moes, zachtwarme appelmoes, smooth with tiny chunks, melting roughage. pure, the way Bob made it, good, clear, round, erg krachtig, smooth, very enjoyable, warm and lively surrounding the tongue, licht, mild, lekkerder dan rauw, in contrast to the smell delicate, well-balanced, mouth-watering. lievelingskleur, Autumn, gras, weilanden, very gezond, the colour and freshness remind me of the Alps, memory of freshness, Summer, Engeland, Wales, bio-industrie, waiting for Nathalie, a good cure for a Winter's cold. macro-biotiek, by an open fire, something I would eat anytime, take small bites, and enjoy longer, lunch, op een heuvelrug in het gras, do it yourself, it can be that simple.

Bob already eight

Bob's Potage   *Bob's seal of approval*

Card 4 (bottom-right)

After replacing my measuring jug (150 ml) with a JOVIA porcelain cup (ARTnr. 340987 HFL 1,95) I continued. polygonic top layer, fantastisch, Oud en Nieuw knallend, Haagse Bluf, 1 deel Blue Nun, 2 delen Exquisite, washing up liquid with gold bits, moet dat goudfolie er in? raar. bitter, fris en zoetig, afwasmiddel. slim shady, bros, bros, bros, bros, bros, sprankelend, schuimig, cleaning, creamy. like egg nog for Summer, dryer than a dog after heat, zeer fris, citroentjesfris, sour 'n bitter first, sweet ever after, het laatste beetje geeft een heel lekker warm gevoel. Kindergarten, partytime, alcoholism for kids, heel zomers en heel geil, twee gele afwashandschoenen, dartelende jonge vrouwen, 6 francs = 2 boules, Sandra from London with a Rubik cube. Spandau ballet remix in Antwerp. by Jeremy Scott lookalike, no comment, hier wordt je zeker een Blue Nun van! fun pub on a Friday, zwaar! aanbevolen, if you can't stand the heat, stay out of the kitchen,

Bob already eight

Bob's sorbet   *Bob's seal of approval*

goodwill
BOB
MAMA, Rotterdam
2001, The Netherlands
A select audience of 80 art lovers was invited to a free conceptual seven-course dinner, hosted by BOB, a creation of goodwill, referring to "BOB" DOBBS (Church of the Sub Genius, a hoax sect). Dinner had been consumed two days earlier by the collaborators and the diners were served each course as a report, with accompanying wine. The seating was arranged so that no-one could see anyone else and the 80 diners were subsequently "forced" to watch an art performance.

Stand
Before World War 2
You had to stand
Sitting is safer
Take a seat

2000 now

2

higher class wore hats
farmers wore caps

71 SEE

18 SEE

11 SEE

79 SEE

5 SEE

1

8

Safety
No more Standing
Seats Are safer
Please Be careful

15

1985

39 people died

17 SEE

18 SEE

COLLECTORS ITEMS

ction Article

Card

18. Sta (195
68 SE
17. Bri
Stadium (193
Be Quick,
(1921), F
16. E. var
Stadium w
R
15. H.A. Mac
Extension Sta
Utrecht (195
August 29,
14. J. Roodenb
Stadium Ajax at
(Watergraafsm
Coloured Plan

82

goodwill, designed with Vanessa van Dam
106 cards for "The Stadium, Architecture for the Masses" exhibition
Netherlands Institute for Architecture, Rotterdam
2000, The Netherlands
106 cards were distributed throughout the exhibition for visitors to
collect; in effect they replaced the catalogue. Exhibition invigilators were
regularly asked, where is card #71? It was in the drinks machine and
visitors had to buy a drink in order to complete their set.

chlorfrei / sans chlore / chlor...

CONTROLLO POSTALE ▲ ABRIR...

▲ HIER OPENEN ▲

/ avec...

* 3S PSZF 516704B *

Alleen voor verzending binnen Nederland

ptt post

pakketzegel

Nederland

Frankering betaald
Nederland

5